Altman's Spring and Summer Fashions Catalog, 1915

B. ALTMAN & CO.

DOVER PUBLICATIONS, INC.
New York

Copyright

Copyright © 1995 by Dover Publications, Inc.
All rights reserved under Pan American and International Copyright Conventions.

Published in Canada by General Publishing Company, Ltd., 30 Lesmill Road, Don Mills, Toronto, Ontario.

Published in the United Kingdom by Constable and Company, Ltd., 3 The Lanchesters, 162–164 Fulham Palace Road, London W6 9ER.

Bibliographical Note

This Dover edition, first published in 1995, is a republication of *B. Altman & Co.: Book of Styles for Spring and Summer*, Number One Hundred Eleven, New York, 1915. The order form originally appearing as pp. 89–90 is here omitted. A Publisher's Note has been written specially for the Dover edition.

Library of Congress Cataloging-in-Publication Data

Book of styles for spring and summer
    Altman's spring and summer fashions catalog, 1915 / B. Altman & Co.
        p.   cm.
    "Republication of B. Altman & Co. : Book of styles for spring and summer, number one hundred eleven, 1915—T.p. verso.
    Includes index.
    ISBN 0-486-28527-8 (pbk.)
    1. Clothing and dress—Catalogs. 2. B. Altman & Co.—Catalogs. I. B. Altman & Co.
II. Title.
TT555.A46 1995
381'.45687'0297471—dc20

                94–44617
                CIP

Manufactured in the United States of America
Dover Publications, Inc., 31 East 2nd Street, Mineola, N.Y. 11501

PUBLISHER'S NOTE

B. ALTMAN & COMPANY was founded in New York City in 1864. A native New Yorker, Benjamin Altman (1840–1913) first opened a small dry goods shop on Third Avenue, near Tenth Street. Although he was only 24 at the time, he possessed a keen business sense and impeccable judgment in selecting merchandise. Over the next nine years, Altman had to relocate his expanding business several times. From 1876 to 1906, he operated his store at Sixth Avenue and Nineteenth Street—on New York's famous Ladies' Mile, an area known for its fashionable retail establishments.

Altman—who foresaw the northward trend of New York's retail trade—began to purchase parcels of land on Fifth Avenue in 1895. Eleven years later, he opened a department store unsurpassed in New York City, perhaps in the world. The building itself was in the Italian Renaissance style, and featured every convenience known to the architecture of the time; a twelve-story addition was constructed in 1914 to accommodate B. Altman's growing clientele. A year after his death, the business that Benjamin Altman had founded fifty years earlier occupied an entire city block, stretching east from Fifth Avenue to Madison Avenue and north from Thirty-fourth Street to Thirty-fifth Street.

The items featured in this 1915 catalog are indicative of the range of merchandise shoppers could find at B. Altman's. The store prided itself on carrying fashions of the latest style and highest quality—though at prices the discriminating middle-class customer could afford. Ready-to-wear suits and dresses (including afternoon mourning frocks and maternity wear), riding habits, tennis skirts, imported Parisian corsets, shoes, boudoir gowns and silk nightcaps were among the offerings to women. Men's fashions included such necessities as motoring robes and flannel trousers, cuffs and collars in "all the newest shapes and variations for the man who keeps abreast with Fashion." Selections were not limited to clothing, however. From these pages everything from golf clubs to Alberta Hair Wavers could be ordered and delivered right to the customer's door.

INDEX

B. Altman & Co.

Fifth Avenue—Madison Avenue
Thirty-fourth and Thirty-fifth Streets
New York

IN the Book of Styles now presented by B. Altman & Co., every effort has been made to describe and illustrate as adequately as possible all merchandise most frequently in demand, and while the fabrics and modes are identical with the Season's offerings in the various departments of the establishment, space does not admit of detailed mention of the great variety of rich materials and of the many rare articles carried in stock.

Out-of-town patrons may have every assurance that all orders and requests for information will receive careful attention, and that the services of a perfectly organized staff of expert shoppers in the Mail Order Department are at all times available.

Any purchase found, upon examination, not entirely satisfactory may be returned for exchange or credit, or, if preferred, money will be refunded.

Book of Styles No. 111—Spring and Summer, 1915

ALL PURCHASES PREPAID

TO ANY PART OF THE UNITED STATES

ALSO TO POSSESSIONS OR FOREIGN COUNTRIES AS FOLLOWS:

All charged or paid purchases (including heavy and bulky shipments) will be forwarded free by mail, express or freight to any point in the United States

All charged or paid purchases not exceeding twenty pounds in weight will be forwarded free by mail to all Territories, Possessions or Foreign Countries where Parcel Post rates apply.

NOTE—The methods of shipment are optional with B. Altman & Co. and no discounts are allowed. All transportation charges for goods sent C. O. D. will be collected on delivery.

1001

1001

1002

1003

1004

1004

For descriptions and prices, see following page

1915

SMART SUITS AND AFTERNOON DRESSES
READY TO WEAR

1101

Garments illustrated on pages 2 to 6, inclusive, can be supplied from regular stock in sizes 34 to 44 inches, bust measurement; and in the materials and colors designated. All skirts average about 42 inches in length, and have basted hems to facilitate adjustment. Should any particular size or color be temporarily out of stock, a few days will be required to fill orders.

1001 SPORTS SUIT, on the season's newest lines; of black and white checked worsted, navy serge or brown mixture. Skirt in circular effect, with plaits at sides. Coat silk lined . . $20.00

1002 TAILORED SUIT, of navy, black or gray vigoreux gabardine. Yoke skirt in circular style, especially adapted for large figures. Coat silk lined. Sizes, 36 to 48 inches, bust measurement $25.00

1003 DRESSY SUIT, of crêpe poplin, in navy, bluet or sand color. Silk collar and self-material belt embroidered with self color and introduction of gilt. Circular skirt repeating the embroidered note in smart side tabs. Coat silk lined $30.00

1004 TAILORED SUIT, in black, navy or white serge. Back of coat smartly belted and plaited. Coat silk lined. Skirt a circular model with modish yoke effect, fastened at side $20.00

1005 FANCY SUIT, of black, navy or sand color silk poplin, with white faille collar; seven-eighths length sleeves. Unique skirt with plaits in front and fancy yoke back. Coat silk lined $32.00

1101 AFTERNOON DRESS, of crêpe de chine; featuring a smart jacket effect, embroidered in self tones, with touches of contrasting color; roll collar of material with over collar and vest of white crêpe. Full circular skirt with graduated tucks. Colors, black, navy, tan or gray $35.00

1005

3

1915

1915

1006

1007

1008

1009

*For descriptions and prices
see following page*

4

1102

1103

1915

1915

WOMEN'S
READY-TO-WEAR
SUITS AND DRESSES

(*Illustrated on pages 4 and 5*)

Please refer to note on page 3 for sizes
carried in stock and for
measurments required

1006 DRESSY TAILORED SUIT,
of navy or black gabardine. Fancy
silk and plain satin finish the collar
and cuffs; cordings of satin and
small buttons add modish touch
at back of coat. The skirt with
plaits at side introduces the popular
flare. Seven-eighths length sleeve.
The coat is silk lined . . $28.00

1007 TAILORED TRAVELING
AND SPORTS SUIT, in navy gabardine, black and white check or
gray tweed. Pockets lend characteristic jauntiness to the circular
skirt. The coat is silk lined $25.00

1008 SEMI-DRESSY SUIT, of
black or navy silk poplin or taffeta,
with collar of white embroidered
faille. A plaited effect at side
gives new flare to the circular skirt.
The coat is silk lined . . $38.00

1009 SEMI-FANCY SUIT, of
bluet, sand or black poplin. Coat
trimmed with moiré silk; skirt in
new circular effect, with two back
plaits. The coat is silk lined $25.00

1102 MATERNITY DRESS of crêpe de chine. Has self-colored moiré collar and
dainty vestee and over-collar of lace in effective combination with the plaited
skirt; waist and sleeves of self material. Colors, black, navy or taupe . $25.00

1103 MOURNING DRESS, for afternoon wear, of black crêpe de chine, smart
in every detail. The waist and sleeves are of self material, with standing
collar; chiffon and point d'esprit contributing a dressy note to the waist front,
and a yoke smartly featuring the full circular skirt $32.00

1103A Same style as above, in black taffeta 28.00

WOMEN'S READY-TO-WEAR DRESSES

Sizes, 34 to 44 inches, bust measurement; skirt lengths average about 42 inches

1104 One-piece Dress, of crepe meteor, in black, navy, tan or gray; standing collar of contrasting shade, also piping on cuffs; vestee of flesh color chiffon; buttons and belt of self material; full skirt finished at bottom with fold of material $22.50

1104A Can also be furnished as an adjustable dress, with elastic band at waist; in black or navy 25.00

1105 Afternoon Dress, of taffeta; waist and collar of material, vestee of white crepe, piping of white and black striped silk, sleeves of white crepe, finished with cuffs of material; circular skirt plaited at yoke, front of skirt button trimmed; can be furnished in black, navy or wistaria 30.00

1106 Afternoon Dress, of charmeuse; waist and girdle of material, fastening to one side with material loops and buttons, guimpe of white dotted net; collar and band around cuff of white charmeuse; sleeves of self color chiffon over white dotted net; circular gored skirt, plaited at center back, fastening at side of front; can be furnished in black, navy or wistaria $25.00

1107 One-piece Evening Gown, of taffeta; waist is surpliced with fancy lace trimming and corsage bouquet; circular skirt with cord shirring forming yoke and finished at bottom with cord; in light blue, maize, pink or white 32.00

6

RIDING HABITS, SPORTS SUITS AND SEPARATE SKIRTS
READY-TO-WEAR

Designed on Perfect-fitting Lines and Carefully Finished Throughout.   Women's Riding Habits,
sizes, 34 to 40 inches, bust measurement; sizes 42 and 44 can be ordered in any style ; Misses' sizes,
14 to 16 years.   Separate Skirts are furnished in waist measurements : 24, 26, 28 and 30 inches

1021 Women's and Misses' Riding Habits, for side saddle ; in tan or jasper linen $10.00

1021A Similar style, in Oxford melton, gray or brown tweed 25.00

1021B Women's and Misses' Long Coat and Breeches ; in cravanetted army khaki, tan or jasper
linen ; breeches reinforced 10.00

1021C Same model, in Oxford melton, gray or brown tweed ; coat lined ; breeches lined with
chamois and reinforced with buckskin 26.00

1021D Same model, in green forestry cravanetted cloth ; unlined 28.00

1021E Child's Riding Habit, paddock effect coat, with breeches ; in tan linen, or cravanetted army
khaki ; sizes, 8 to 14 . . . . $9.00

1021F Same style as No. 1021E, in brown or gray Irish homespun or tan
covert cloth ; coat satin lined 17.50

1021G Separate Breeches, in brown or black sateen 2.45

1022 Women's and Misses' Combination Sports or Riding Suits ; in tan
linen or cravanetted army khaki, with shell skirt, buttons down front
and fasteners down back 10.00

1022A Breeches, to match above suit 4.50

1022B Same style as No. 1022, in brown or gray mixture ; coat lined . . . 25.00

1022C Same style as above, in green forestry cravanetted cloth 25.00

1022D Breeches, to match the above styles, lined or unlined, reinforced
with chamois and buckskin $9.50

1022E Shell Skirt, buttons at front and fasteners
down back ; in gray or brown tweed, also
Oxford melton 7.25

1022F Safety or Divided Skirt, in Oxford melton . 9.75

1022G Same as above, in tan linen, or cravenetted
army khaki 5.50

1023 Sports Skirts, of bluet, rose, white or sand
golfine, white serge with black hairline stripe,
black and white check worsted, navy or white
serge, gray or brown tweed 5.75

1024 Circular Flare Dress Skirt, of black taffeta,
with shirred and plaited yoke effect 8.75

1025 Tailored Skirt, black or blue wool poplin, or black and white check worsted ;
in circular effect, with side fastening,
special at 3.85

1026 Tailored Skirt, on smart lines ; in black or
blue serge, also black and white check
worsted $6.25

1027 Plaited Crepe de Chine Skirt, not
illustrated, white or black ; special 5.35

1028 Full Flare Skirt, not illustrated, of black
or navy serge, with short yoke, fastened
at side front ; especially designed for large
figures ; sizes, 30 to 37 inches, waist
measurement 6.25

1022

1021

1023

1024

1025

1026

1915 1915

WOMEN'S
YOUTHFUL
COTTON
FROCKS

1201
1202
1203
1205
1204

Embodying the Season's Newest Features, at moderate prices
Sizes, 34 to 40 inches, bust measurement; sizes 42 and 44
ordered upon request; skirt lengths average about 40 inches

1201   White Cotton Voile Dress, embroidery trimmed, and finished
       with black moiré silk belt having sash ends; touch of black
       repeated on collar $8.75

1202   Cotton Voile Shirt-waist Frock, in white or the new peach
       shade; designed in favored tier skirt effect, daintily finished
       with hemstitching; white organdie furnishes the plaited collar,
       revers and cuffs, and black velvet, the belt 10.75

1203   White Embroidered Marquisette Dress, with effective trim-
       mings of filet lace and white moiré ribbon 18.00

1204   Dainty Frock, of white organdie; another tier skirt effect
       model, with embroidered edging; waist has tucked yoke, front
       and back, with dainty embroidered edge and trimmings, and
       coral silk belt for effective touch of color 11.50

1205   White Cotton Voile Dress, exquisitely hand-embroidered,
       hemstitched and tucked; introducing filet lace motifs in waist,
       and neatly belted in the plaited material 15.00

WOMEN'S
YOUTHFUL
COTTON
FROCKS

(Continued)

Sizes 34 to 40 inches, bust measurement; sizes 42 and 44 ordered upon request; skirt lengths average about 40 inches

1211   Cotton Batiste Dress, in light blue or champagne color; prettily tucked waist with three-ruffled skirt tucked to correspond; black and white banding in blocked patterns lends refreshing trimming note, with lace for collar and sleeves and black velvet ribbon for belt . . $11.50

1212   Cotton Voile Shirt-waist Dress, a striking model in the much favored black and white stripes; the skirt plaited on sides for added fullness, suède belt, button trimmed, and collar and cuffs daintily edged with lace 6.50

1213   One-piece Street Frock, of white linen, with smart plaited skirt having a fashionably contrasting top of russet or blue linen; collar and cuffs of white embroidered organdie, and belt of white kid 7.75

1214   Dress, of white linen; the collar, cuffs and belt trimmed with pearl buttons, carrying the color note of blue or pink; waist attractively hand-embroidered in front .   12.50

1215   Dainty Blue Linen Frock, fashionably pocketed; combined with white and blue dotted voile sleeves and underbody; collar embroidered and pearl button trimmed; may also be ordered in pink, tan or all white   10.75

WOMEN'S WAISTS AND TAILORED COTTON SPORTS SKIRTS

Waist sizes: 34, 36, 38, 40, 42 and 44 inches, bust measurement

Skirt sizes as follows: Waistbands, 28, 30 and 32 inches; lengths, 38 and 40 inches, with 4-inch basted hems

1221 Skirt, of striped beach cloth (cotton mixture), in tan shade; trimmed with pearl buttons, one tailored pocket, bias band round bottom of skirt $5.75

1221A Same model, in white cotton velvet corduroy 5.75

1222 Skirt, of white cotton cordelais; pointed yoke front, four-inch straight yoke back, pearl buttons at top . . 2.75

1223 Skirt, of beach cloth (cotton mixture), in tan color; finished in front with buttons, yoke from sides and back with tucks below 5.75

1223A Same model, in white ramie linen 5.75

1224 Skirt, of white cotton cordelais; finished with pocket, pearl buttons top and bottom of skirt 2.75

1224A Same model, in white ratine (cotton fabric) 4.75

1225 Tan Beach Cloth (cotton mixture), opened all way

down front; fancy tab finished belt in back, finished with pearl buttons and two pockets $5.75

1301 Blouse, of handkerchief linen, in highly favored stripes, with convenient convertible collar; colors, blue and white, tan and white or pink and white 3.00

1302 Handkerchief Linen Blouse, with soft collar and cuffs of piqué and finished with a side pocket in white only 3.00

1303 Blouse, of fancy voile; convertible collar finished with military loops and buttons 3.50

1304 Smart Sports Blouse, of white linen, with convertible collar, featuring the new suspender effect 2.45

1305 Interesting Voile Model, in white or pale pink with the new half raglan sleeves; tucks afford front and back trimming, the high collar being finished at neck with a moiré bow 3.75

WOMEN'S, MISSES' AND CHILDREN'S BATHING SUITS, ETC.

Women's Bathing Suits can be furnished in sizes, 34 to 44 inches; also any of the above models in Misses' sizes, 14, 16 and 18 years.
Several styles are illustrated above, but others can be supplied in Mohair, Satins and Taffeta Silks, ranging in price from $7.50 to $50.00

1400 Woman's Black Satin Bathing Suit; collar, vest and cuffs of corded satin; yoke on skirt piped and trimmed with pearl buttons, including combination $15.50
1401 Fancy Rubber Bathing Cap, finished with a bunch of berries of rubber on both sides 2.25
1402 Bathing Boots, of white canvas, strapped in tan or black leather; especially adapted for beach trotting 1.65
1403 Woman's Black Satin Suit, high waisted model; smartly trimmed with corded silk and fancy buttons, including combination 13.75
1404 Bathing Bonnet, of rubberized black satin, with facing of contrasting colors and trimmed with roses 4.50
1405 Misses' Suit, of navy blue mohair; collar, sleeves and belt trimmed with Roman striped silk; skirt plaited; separate combination 6.75

1405A Same style as No. 1405, in women's; mohair, in black or navy $7.75
1405B Also in black satin 12.00
1406 Bathing Hat, of rubberized satin, in the smart shades . . . 1.50
1407 Woman's one-piece Swimming Suit, of black jersey; colored piping and buttons 6.00
1408 Rubber Cap, with contrasting color band and tassels . . . 1.75
1409 Child's Suit, of navy blue jersey, trimmed with red braid; separate skirt of navy blue mohair; sizes, 4 to 10 years . . . 2.95
1410 Women's Mohair Suit, especially adapted for swimming; white and black stripe trimming, with combination 4.85
1411 Bathing Hat, of rubberized satin; colors, black, green, red or purple 2.75
1412 Misses' Suit, of navy blue mohair, with piping of white piqué; separate mohair bloomers 3.85
1413 Diving Cap, of heavy rubber 60

In addition to the illustrations, a full line of Women's, Misses' and Children's Bathing Suits, also a complete assortment of Bathing Accessories are carried in stock

B. ALTMAN & CO. NEW YORK

WOMEN'S BLOUSES

Sizes carried in stock are 34, 36, 38, 40, 42 and 44, bust measure, with the exception of Colored Silk and Chiffon Waists, in which sizes larger than 40 inches can be ordered specially. Ten days are required to fill orders for garments which are not in stock

1310 Cream Lace Blouse, lined with white chiffon, finished with fancy buttons, standing collar to back, long sleeves; can be ordered with three-quarter sleeves . . $13.75

1311 Chiffon Blouse, tucked model, bands of lace under chiffon back and front and lace vest bolero effect; in black and white, navy and white or gray and white; can be ordered with three-quarter sleeves if desired . . 12.50

1312 Embroidered Crepe de Chine Blouse, convertible collar faced with white crepe de chine; in flesh color, navy,

white or black $6.25

1313 French Crepe Blouse, in white or flesh color, daintily tucked and embroidered; high standing collar finished with tie; smart cuffs 9.75

1314 French Crepe Blouse, embroidered and lace trimmed, lined with chiffon; in navy and white, pink and white or black and white 9.50

1315 Embroidered French Crepe Blouse, bolero effect, emb. organdie collar and cuffs; in flesh color, white or navy 8.50

1915

1316 1317 1318 1319 1320 1321

WOMEN'S BLOUSES—(Continued)

Sizes carried in stock are: 34, 36, 38, 40, 42 and 44 inches
bust measurement

1316 White Voile Blouse, trimmed with embroidery and lace, clusters of fine tucks on sleeves and shoulder; new shoulder sleeves; can be ordered specially with three-quarter sleeves $3.50

1317 White Hand-embroidered Voile Blouse; filet lace down front and on collar and cuffs; can be ordered with three-quarter or long sleeves 4.75

1318 White Embroidered Voile Blouse, with open veining throughout, convertible collar, long sleeves 4.85

1319 Embroidered Voile Blouse, daintily trimmed with lace, low flat collar; in pale pink, bisque or white; can be ordered with long or three-quarter sleeves $4.50

1320 Figured White Voile Blouse, with organdie collar lace trimmed; black tie, long sleeves 5.00

1321 White Voile Blouse, front trimmed with dainty embroidery and fine tucks, collar and cuffs of organdie, three-quarter or long sleeves 1.85

13

1915

1915

1325

1326

1327

1328

1329

1330

WOMEN'S BLOUSES—(Continued)

Sizes carried in stock are: 34, 36, 38, 40, 42 and 44 inches, bust measurement

1325 Striped Wash Silk Blouse, collar can be worn high or low; in pink and white, blue and white, brown and white $4.50

1326 Jap Silk Blouse, standing collar to back, V-neck with revers, two rows of tucking down front; in black or white   3.75

1326A Same model as above, in messaline or taffeta silk   .   .   4.50

1327 Crepe de Chine Blouse, with smocking at shoulder; convertible collar; in maize, flesh color, white, black or navy   6.50

1328 Striped Wash Silk Blouse, finished with pearl buttons, convertible collar; in white and black, white and blue, white and tan $3.00

1329 Chiffon Taffeta Military Blouse, in white with navy blue braiding or white with black braiding   .   .   .   8.50

1330 Crepe de Chine Blouse, yoke effect back and front; eyelet embroidery, convertible collar; in bisque or white   5.50

1915
1333
1334
1335
1336
1337
1338

WOMEN'S BLOUSES—(Continued)

Sizes carried in stock are : 34, 36, 38, 40, 42 and 44 inches, bust measurement

1333 White Opaline Sports Shirt, yoke effect ; box plaits and pockets, fastens front, long sleeves, high neck . . . $2.90

1334 White Voile Blouse, with standing collar to back ; V-neck, finished with band of moiré ribbon ; tucked jabot front with embroidered dots and fancy cuffs . . 5.00

1335 Voile Blouse, box-plaited from yoke effect, daintily embroidered ; finished with linen collar, cuffs and vestee ; in pale pink, pale blue, bisque or white ; can be ordered with three-quarter sleeves 3.75

1336 Voile Blouse, tucked model ; new shoulder sleeves, low collar, turnback cuffs, fastens front ; in bisque, white, or shell pink ; can be had with three-quarter or long sleeves $1.90

1337 Striped Linen Blouse, convertible collar faced with white linen, finished with large pearl buttons ; in blue and white or black and white 5.00

1338 Voile Blouse, daintily embroidered front ; finished with hemstitching throughout, embroidered organdie collar and cuffs ; in bisque, pale pink or white . . . 5.00

15

1915   1915

1501
1502
1503
1504
1505

WOMEN'S OUTERGARMENTS

Women's Outergarments can be furnished in the following sizes: 34, 36, 38, 40, 42 and 44 inches
Lengths as mentioned in the various descriptions.   A few days required to furnish sizes which may not be in stock

1501   Tan and Green Mixed Tweed Showerproof and Travel
Coat, yoke lined, buttoning high to the neck or may be worn
open; set-in sleeves attached at large arm size with cuffs, slit
pockets; length, 50 inches $16.50

1502   White Chinchilla Coat, unlined; becomingly belted all
around and displaying the smart flare skirt; a soft collar
permits of high or low adjustment; large armholes feature the
set-in sleeves, with cuffs; length, 41 inches 25.00

1503   Black or Navy Blue Wool Bengaline Coat, lined
throughout in self color silk; with black silk bengaline collar,
slit pockets, set-in sleeves with cuffs; self revers; length, 44 in. 19.50

1504   Tan Linen Duster, for traveling, having exceptionally smart
straight back caught at loose side plaits by a button-finished
belt; raglan sleeves; standing collar, which may be worn
high or low, and convenient slit pockets; length, 52 inches . $5.75

1504A Can be furnished for Misses in 14-year size; length, 48 inches;
16 and 18-year sizes; length, 50 inches 5.75

1505   Tan Covert Box Coat, in 38-inch length; lined throughout
in self-color silk; collar, patch pockets and back of yoke
appropriately stitched and raglan sleeves finished with button-
trimmed cuffs 17.50

16

1915
1915

1510   1511   1512   1513   1514

WOMEN'S OUTERGARMENTS—(Continued)

Women's Outergarments can be furnished in the following sizes: 34, 36, 38, 40, 42 and 44 inches
Lengths as mentioned in the various descriptions.   A few days required to furnish sizes which may not be in stock

1510   **Tan Tussah and Black Satin Reversible Semi-Wrap,**
in modish Empire effect at back ; the set-in sleeves with cuffs,
flare skirt and flat collar are smartly augmented by dressy revers
formed at the opened fronts ; length, 49 inches $28.00

1511   **Gray and Black Plaid Tweed Coat,** with 50-inch straight
back fashionably shortening toward the front : yoke also
sleeves lined with gray silk, flare skirt, wide belt extending
across back and terminating at pockets in front ; sleeves set
in at modish large arm size, finished with pointed cuffs ; standing turnover collar of black silk bengaline, introducing a band
of self material 22.50

1512   **Tan Palm Beach Cloth Travel or Motor Coat,** embodying the straight loose back, smartly belted ; slit pockets,

sleeves set into the new large armholes, turnback cuffs and
standing collar to be worn high or low, finished with pearl
buttons ; in practical 54-inch length $9.75

1513   **Silk Poplin Wrap,** in black or sand color, featuring a silk-
lined yoke back and front : set-in sleeves with cuffs, side-
pointed ripple skirt and standing collar with revers appropriately fastened with a bow of self material ; 41 inches in back   35.00

1514   **Light Weight Gray Wool Tweed Coat,** unlined,
combining newest features with its practical pos-
sibilities ; the set-in sleeves carry the season's popular
finish cuff, slit pockets are provided and the flare
collar may also be worn high ; length, 53 inches ; at
the special price of 12.50

17

1915   1915

1602

1601

1603

1604

1605

1606

MORNING TUB FROCKS AND MAIDS' DRESSES

Furnished in sizes 36 to 44 inches, bust measurement

TRIM LINES AND SMART FEATURES IN PRACTICAL MATERIALS

1601   Maid's Dress, of black or gray cotton alpaca, with collar and cuffs of white hemstitched lawn $3.00

1601A Same style, in check or blue chambray 2.25

1602   Tea Apron, of fine lawn; lace and ribbon trimmed . . 1.00

1602A Lawn Bow Cap; same may be untied 12

1603   Morning Dress, of white piqué; collar effectively embroidered and waist trimmed with pearl buttons . . 3.95

1604   Morning Dress, of linene, with hand-embroidered collar, cuffs and vest of soft white basket

cloth; yoke skirt; black velvet ribbon belt and tie; colors, pink, light blue and lavender; special, at $3.00

1604A Same style, in striped madras; colors, blue and white, lavender and white or gray and white 3.00

1605   Morning Dress, of striped madras, with dainty collar and cuffs of white organdie; colors, blue, lavender or gray 2.25

1606   Morning Dress, of ramie cloth, with white collar and cuffs and contrasting trimmings of black velvet; colors, pink, blue, amethyst, rose or tan 3.95

1609 1610 1611

1612

1419

1420

1418

1417

1416

BOUDOIR GOWNS, CAPS AND NEGLIGEES

Boudoir Gowns and Negligees are furnished in sizes 36, 38 and 42 inches, bust measurement, but may be ordered in any size desired; or should other materials be preferred, samples and estimates will be furnished upon request.

1416 Boudoir Negligee, of crêpe de chine; silk lined; pink, light blue, lavender, rose, cadet, white or black; daintily hand-emb., finished with hemstitched border $15.50

1417 House Gown, Empire model in crêpe de chine; waist hand-embroidered in self color, and skirt accordion plaited on an elastic belt; white collar and cuffs hemstitched; colors, pink, blue, lavender, rose or cadet $6.75

1418 House Gown, of crêpe de chine; in pale pink, light blue, lavender or black; Empire model jacket, daintily hand-embroidered and lace trimmed; skirt softly box plaited on an elastic band $14.50

1419 Negligee, of white embroidered cotton voile; silk lined throughout; shawl collar and dainty Valenciennes lace finish $6.75

1420 Boudoir Coat, of albatross, deep shawl collar and cuffs of white lingerie; in pink, light blue or lavender $7.50

1420A Same style, as illustration No. 1420 in French flannel; colors, pink, light blue or lavender $9.50

1609. Dressy Cap, of silk shadow lace over chiffon lining; edged with double ruffle of plaited lace, and finished with simple ribbon garniture $2.00

1610 Tucked Net Cap, in quaint bonnet style; shadow lace, ribbon motifs and chiffon rosebud trimming contribute their dainty shades of pink, blue and white $1.85

1611 Net Cap, Valenciennes insertion and edge, motif of lace with ribbon buds and ribbon band ending in front; streamers are combined in piquant charm $1.65

1612 Crêpe de Chine Cap, in white, blue, pink or lavender; wired side points and crown of dotted net, scalloped ruffle of plain net at front and back, with hemstitching and ribbon rosettes for dressy finish $1.00

MISSES' AND JUNIORS' APPAREL

Misses' and Juniors' sizes range as follows: 14 years, 32 inches bust measure, 24½ inches waist, 36 inches skirt length; 16 years, 34 inches bust measure, 25½ inches waist, 38 inches skirt length; 18 years, 36 inches bust measure, 26½ inches waist, 39 inches skirt length. Junior sizes, 15 years, 32 inches bust measure, 25½ inches waist, 33 inches skirt length; 17 years, 33 inches bust measure, 26½ inches waist, 35 inches skirt length

1701 Tailor-made Junior Suit, of basket weave wool material, on semi-Empire lines; with leather belt fastened at waist with large metal buckle; sleeves, front and sides of coat trimmed with inlaid silk ball buttons; satin over collar; panel yoke skirt with side flare; in navy, beige and new blue; can be specially ordered in all white or black; sizes, 15 and 17 years $22.50

1702 Tailor-made Junior Suit, in the new belted model, with slight gathering from semi-yoke at front and across back; wide box plait at center of back, strapped patch pockets on coat and side of skirt; flare skirt finished at waist with detachable belt; in navy serge, black and white check, also tan mixtures; can be specially ordered in white or black serge; sizes, 15 and 17 years $19.50

1703 Street or Outing Coat, for junior girls in a three-quarter flare model; finished at waist with patent leather belt, bias buttonholes and inlaid silk

collar, which can be worn standing or sailor style; fancy black and white check with brown or green overstripe or navy blue diagonal; 15 and 17 years $9.75

1703A Suspender Skirt, with deep hip yoke and two vest pockets at front of yoke; center seam trimmed with fancy buttons at top, wide inlaid plaits and entire garment completed with fashionable bretelles; navy, white or black serge, also black and white check; sizes, 15 and 17 years $7.75

1703B Same as above, in white piqué 4.75

1704 Junior Coat, in semi-high waisted model, for street or outing wear; back falls in soft fullness held at waist with wide split belt, fastening at back with fancy buttons; split piped collar, can be worn flare or lay down; coat silk lined throughout; in sand, or navy gabardine; all white or all black can be specially ordered; sizes, 15 and 17 years $19.50

1705 Tailor-made Suit, in entirely new panel front model; coat is finished at waistline with fancy leather belt and trimmed with fancy buttons and striped silk collar and revers, back of coat is finished with wide box plait from beltline; skirt is new flare model with wide inlaid panels each side of front; black and white check worsted, also beige and Copenhagen gabardine; sizes, 14, 16 and 18 years; navy blue, all black, all white or junior sizes can be specially ordered $29.50

MISSES' AND JUNIORS' APPAREL
(Continued)

Please refer to note on opposite page for sizes carried in stock and for measurements required

1710 Tailor-made Suit, for street, travel or sports wear, of medium ribbed golf cord; coat entirely silk lined, soft hanging belted model with patch pockets, three-button single-breasted front trimmed with ball bone buttons; skirt is an entirely new style with two patch pockets, the front gores shaping into a belt across the gathered back; colors, sand, rose or Copenhagen; white and other shades can be specially ordered; sizes, 14, 16 and 18 years $22.50

1711 Fancy Tailor-made Suit, in short coat model, trimmed at waist with small leather straps and metal buttons across front and back; bottom of coat is finished at back with fan plaits at sides of hips; collar and cuffs are inlaid with combination faille silk; flare skirt with umbrella seams at sides, finished at waist with detachable fancy cut belt; colors, navy serge or black and white check worsted; sizes, 14, 16 and 18 years $28.00

1712 Tailor-made Suit, on original lines; coat has semi-belted sides with deep flaps and graceful flare, two-button front with notch collar and combination silk over collar; skirt has box plait at each side; flaps at waist harmonize with coat; navy serge, green or beige gabardine; can be ordered in other shades; also in all white, black or black and white check; 14, 16, 18 yrs. $24.00

1713 Tailor-made Suit, with coat cut on entirely new lines and lined with silk peau de cygne; panel seamed front finished at waist with belt from sides around back, belt has oval pearl slide buckle center of back with patch pockets at sides, back of coat is made with scallop yoke and two box plaits to waistline; picot edged washable piqué over collar; skirt is a very stylish flare model with patch pockets in front and yoke back, finished with belt to harmonize with coat; sizes, 14, 16 and 18 years; in navy blue serge, black and white check worsted or gray homespun mixture . . . $19.50

1713A The above model can be ordered specially in black serge, $19.50; or white serge $21.00

1714 Novel Tailor Suit, with fan-plaited sides from waist on jacket and finished at waist with narrow self belt; revers and pointed collar and pointed cuffs are trimmed with corded silk; skirt has inlaid panels of fan plaits at sides to harmonize with jacket and is finished at waist with self strap and metal buckle; colors, navy blue, covert or reseda whipcords; can be specially ordered in all white or black; sizes, 14, 16 and 18 years $35.00

B. ALTMAN & CO., NEW YORK

1915   1915

1717   1718   1719   1720   1721

MISSES' AND JUNIORS' APPAREL
(Continued)

Please refer to note on page 20 for sizes carried in stock and for measurements required

1717 Luncheon and Afternoon Frock, of summer weight faille silk, with hand-embroidered waist and sash tab; star pointed silk collar with inner collar of embroidered plaited batiste; fancy suède belt and gathered flare skirt, finished at hips and bottom with self covered cord; colors, navy with sand, sand with navy and green with sand; sizes, 14, 16 and 18 years $28.50

1718 Afternoon Dress, of heavy crepe de chine, back and front of self material; skirt trimmed with a deep tuck with corded edge; the shirt bosom yoke is of gathered square mesh silk net, with gathered point collar to match; two self ornaments trim the front of blouse; colors, sand, Copenhagen or rose; can be specially ordered all white, black and other shades; sizes, 14, 16 and 18 years 24.50

1719 Afternoon Frock, in composé effect, with Georgette crepe blouse and silk charmeuse skirt and girdle; vest is of combination crepe with over collar to match; front of blouse, also girdle tabs are hand-embroidered; two corded bias folds finish the skirt; in navy, sand or rose; other shades can be specially ordered; sizes, 14, 16 and 18 years $22.50

1720 Afternoon Dress, of crepe de chine; chiffon sleeves, collar and cuffs; waist on Empire lines with combination vest and small pendant ornaments; skirt is flare model, plaits at waist and cluster tucks above hem; Copenhagen, navy or rose; all white or black and other colors can be specially ordered; sizes, 15 and 17 years   19.50

1721 Misses' Afternoon Gown, of fine quality crepe meteor, with satin edged chiffon over collar, vestee and cuffs; blouse hand-embroidered; cord girdle and hand-embroidered ornament; skirt is a scallop yoke model with deep soft plaited flare; a corded hem finishes the bottom of skirt; colors, pearl gray, navy and green; can be specially ordered all black, all white and other colors; sizes, 14, 16, and 18 years 24.50

22

MISSES' AND JUNIORS' APPAREL—(Continued)

Please refer to note on page 20 for sizes carried in stock and for measurements required

1725 Junior Evening Frock, of chiffon taffeta, in high-waisted model with decolette inlay and sleeve caps of embroidered net; bodice and girdle edged with French folds and finished with dainty flowers; the gathered circular skirt is finished with deep scallops trimmed with silk folds to harmonize with waist; colors, maize, pink or light blue; sizes, 15 and 17 years . . . $19.50

1726 Dainty Evening Frock, of soft-finished satin with crushed satin girdle; a graceful draping of combination velvet ribbon with small roses on the pendants gives a decidedly French touch; antique mesh lace forms the dainty sleeve and inlay across bust and back; skirt is a full-gathered model finished with three bias folds; colors, flesh pink, light blue or maize; sizes, 14, 16 and 18 years 26.00

1727 Evening Dress, of high luster soft satin with high waistline and crush bodice, finished with dainty wild flower bouquets; the soft draped waist is finished with embroidered metal lace across front, back and graceful sleeve; hem of skirt is finished with the fashionable covered cable cord; colors, Nile green, flesh pink or white; sizes, 14, 16 and 18 years $22.50

1728 Evening Frock, of silk taffeta, on the fashionable Empire lines; umbrella gored flare skirt with bodice of silver-beaded net; square decolette front and back with ruffle sleeve and large Japanese bow of silk net; large velvet rose completes the corsage; colors, pink, light blue or white; sizes, 14, 16 and 18 years . . . 29.50

1729 Misses' Evening Gown, of soft taffeta silk, with puff Empire bodice; girdled at bust with a twist of velvet ribbon and finished with a dainty bouquet; short cap sleeve is of net with metal embroidery; skirt is a gracefully hanging circular flare model; colors, pink, light blue or white; sizes, 14, 16 and 18 years . . . 18.75

The above models can be specially ordered in Junior or Misses' sizes, also in any other colors which may be desired, requiring about two weeks to complete

23

MISSES' AND JUNIORS' APPAREL—(Continued)

Please refer to note on page 20 for sizes carried in stock and for measurements required

1735   Every-day Dress, of natural pongee, with contrasting collar and cuffs of faille silk; body and skirt has corded braid trimming and pockets are also embroidered; the waist is finished with suède leather belt; colors, natural trimmed with green or brown; sizes, 14, 16 and 18 yrs $19.50

1736   Tailor-made Dress, of fine quality worsted, trimmed with ivory ball buttons; white faille silk collar, which can be worn V or high neck; waist finished with detachable belt, forming circular panel effect back of skirt; skirt has two Russian patch pockets and is finished with four rows stitching above hem; colors, navy blue serge, also black and white check; all black can be specially ordered; sizes, 14, 16 and 18 years 9.75

1737   The New Three-piece Dress, with coatee and skirt of golf cord and washable white voile waist; jacket has slit sides joined under arm with stitched-on straps, finished with large pearl buttons; skirt has large flap side pockets and is finished with silk girdle to match bow on front of waist; waist has hemstitched collar and cuffs; colors, rose, white or putty; sizes, 14, 16 and 18 years . . . 22.50

1738   The New Three-piece Dress, with separate silk crepe waist finished with hemstitched organdie collar and cuffs; the coatee or bolero is also separate and is trimmed with metal buttons; skirt is a yoke model with two pockets in yoke; in navy serge with striped waist or white serge with white waist; sizes, 14, 16 and 18 years $22.50

1739   Tailor-made Semi-fancy Dress, of fine twill serge, with embroidered collar, crossover belt and pointed tabs at back of waist; front of waist and sleeves finished with self ball buttons; entirely new model skirt, fashioned on Empire lines; in navy, white and sand color; sizes, 14, 16 and 18 years 19.50

MISSES' AND JUNIORS' APPAREL

(Continued)

Please refer to note on page 20 for sizes
carried in stock and for measurments required

1745 Street or Travel Coat, cut on loose box lines, with wide flare at bottom; unlined; new soft crush collar, with velvet under facing, which can be worn military or turned down; slit side pockets; in navy blue, cheviot, also brown or gray mixture; sizes, 14, 16 and 18 years $13.50

1746 Outing Coat, of summer weight golf cord; lined throughout with silk peau de cygne; new convertible collar, which can be worn flat, flare or buttoned to throat; graceful loose back, finished at waist with buttonhole strap and trimmed with self material large disk buttons; colors, rose, white, maize; Copenhagen and other shades can be especially ordered, also junior pattern at same price; sizes, 14, 16 and 18 years $15.50

1747 Misses' Street or Outing Coat, trimmed with patch pockets; belt all round, split at sides and trimmed with large fancy buttons; new shape convertible flare collar; can be worn open or buttoned to neck; colors, black and white check with green hairline, black and white check with brown hairline, navy blue diagonal; can be specially ordered in black; sizes, 14, 16 and 18 years . . . $10.50

1748 Loose Box Model English Top Coat, made of twilled covert or gray mixtures, lined throughout with silk peau de cygne; bias slashed side pockets and entire garment finished with flat tailor stitching; can be worn buttoned to neck or open front; sizes, 14, 16 and 18 years . . $16.50

1749 Coat, for outing and street wear, in plaited flare model belted all round, with velvet ornament at back, velvet collar and metal buttons complete the trimming; colors, black and white check, covert or navy blue cheviot; can be specially ordered in black; sizes, 14, 16 and 18 years . $9.75

1749A Same style as above, can be ordered in white serge $10.75

25

1915 1915

1755 1756 1757 1758 1759

1760

MISSES' AND JUNIORS' APPAREL
(Continued)

Please refer to note on page 20 for sizes carried in stock and for measurements required

1755 Two-piece Dress, of two-tone striped washable crêpe, with separate waist of hand-embroidered washable voile; embroidery on collar and cuffs to match stripe of dress; soft flare skirt, finished at waistline with bayadere striped self belt; small pearl buttons at front and on belt complete the simple trimming; colors, white with gold, white with Copenhagen, white with green; sizes, 14, 16 and 18 years $12.50

1756 Regulation Sailor Suit, in imported linen, with laced back and drop front middy skirt; hand-embroidered crow-foot pockets on yoke of waist and skirt; hand-embroidered emblems on collar and sleeves; colors, cadet blue, also white; sizes, 14, 16 and 18 years; can be specially ordered in junior sizes 7.75

1756A Same model can be furnished in navy serge, also white serge, at 9.50

1757 Washable Dress, of striped corded tissue with hand-embroidered organdie vest, collar and cuffs; hand-embroidered dots and arrows on box plaits at front of skirt; pearl buttons down front and self material belt comprise the balance of trimming of this very dainty frock; colors, Copenhagen, pink or green stripes; sizes, 14, 16 and 18 years; black stripe can be specially ordered 6.75

1758 Tailor Dress, of ramie linen, with fancy patch pocket on blouse and skirt, trimmed with flat pearl buttons; piqué slashed cuffs and collar, finished at V-neck with satin ribbon tie; detachable belt of self material; colors, Copenhagen, rose or white; sizes, 14, 16 and 18 years; can be specially ordered in junior sizes 6.50

1759 Morning Frock, of striped crêpe, with hand-embroidered voile collar and vest; skirt with hip plaits falling into fullness; self material detachable belt; colors, white with Copenhagen, rose or gold stripes; sizes, 14, 16 and 18 years 5.75

1760 Dress, of cotton crêpe, with hemstitched box plaits front and back of waist and skirt; voile collar and cuffs. The graceful moiré girdle and combination hand-crochet buttons on sleeves and down the front complete the trimming of this morning frock; colors, rose, Copenhagen or white; sizes, 14 16 and 18 years 14.50

1915 · 1765 · 1766 · 1767 · 1768 · 1769 · 1770 · 1915

MISSES' AND JUNIORS' APPAREL

(Continued)

Please refer to note on page 20 for sizes carried in stock and for measurements required

1765   Washable White Net Dress, over net foundation; waist is V-neck front and back and trimmed with embroidered bands; the vest, sleeves and full skirt are made with tucks with two rows of hemstitching above the tucks on skirt; wide moiré girdle and tab; white, pink or blue girdles; sizes, 14, 16 and 18 years . $15.75

1766   Dress, of embroidered white blond net over a plaited net foundation; jacket is a bolero effect trimmed with filet lace, wide silk girdle; waist and skirt are finished with a double picot edged ruffle in waved design; lace collar and a dainty draping of black velvet baby ribbon; colors, pink, blue or white Dresden girdles; all white ribbon can be specially ordered; sizes, 14, 16 and 18 years 29.50

1767   Washable Dress, of ramie linen, with combination collar, cuffs and belt; inlaid panel pocket each side of front of skirt, finished with hemstitching; pearl buttons down the front with two rows of hemstitching complete the tailor effect; collar can be worn buttoned to neck or turned down; colors, Copenhagen, rose, tan or white; sizes, 14, 16 and 18 years 9.75

1768   Dainty Dress, of fine washable white voile, with hand-embroidery; fine hairline tucks on waist and front of skirt, hem is finished with a hemstitch with hand-embroidery above, collar is also hand-embroidered and small crochet buttons finish the front; wide moiré ribbon girdle in Copenhagen, rose or white; sizes, 14, 16 and 18 years; can be specially ordered in junior sizes 10.50

1769   Washable Dress, of white corded voile, with full skirt hemstitched; inlaid yoke effect; hand-crocheted buttons down front; collar, cuffs and vestee are hand-embroidered, also hand-embroidered loops at yoke of skirt; moiré silk girdle in Copenhagen, rose or gold, fastening at side with crochet buttons; sizes, 14, 16 and 18 years 17.50

1770   Empire Model Misses' Dress, of fine quality washable white voile; waist of embroidered net, with over bodice of embroidered batiste; embroidered net flare to sleeve; skirt is shirred at waistline and finished with hem and two hemstitched tucks above; sizes, 14, 16 and 18 years 16.50

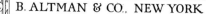

MISSES' AND JUNIORS' SEPARATE WAISTS AND SKIRTS
Sizes, 14, 16 and 18 years

1775 Striped Taffeta Waist, with black moiré stock collar and linen turnover, cuffs are made to match collar; the new set-in short yoke sleeve is also a distinguishing new feature; colors, white and Copenhagen, navy and white, putty and blue; all black can be ordered $5.50
1776 Waist, of white washable voile; collar and cuffs finished with hemstitched handkerchief hem, front is embroidered and trimmed with button-through crochet buttons; back is tucked in cluster pin tucks $1.95
1777 Waist, of fine quality crêpe de chine; combination hemstitched collar, tie and cuffs; the collar and tie is in one-piece scarf effect, fastened across front with tab and finished with pearl buttons; colors, white and flesh, white and blue, flesh and white; can be specially ordered in all white and all black . . $5.75
1778 Waist, of white washable voile, with embroidered front, collar and cuffs; back, front and sleeves are daintily trimmed with cluster pin tucks; small pearl buttons down front and on collar $2.25
1779 Misses' Shirt, in striped handkerchief linen; hemstitched white linen band down front and around collar and cuffs; collar can be worn high or low; front of waist is trimmed with washable crochet olives and loops; colors, rose, Copenhagen, lavender or black stripes $2.85
1780 White Linen Tailored Shirt, with new V-neck revers and soft turnover collar, which can be worn closed or open at neck; two patch pockets and iridescent pearl buttons complete the detail of this strictly tailored waist $2.35
1781 Three-gored Flare Worsted Skirt, with rever patch pockets; waist is

finished with wide detachable self belt with crossover fastening at front; navy or white serge, also covert $5.75
1782 Suspender Skirt, in worsted materials; fastening down front under fish-fin plait; large patch pockets, finished with tailor buttons; suspender is also trimmed with patch watch pocket; colors, black and white check, blue serge, also white serge $7.50
1783 Sports Skirt, of light weight golf cord; slash pockets each side of front; a novel belt has flaps buttoning over pockets and fastened with self color buttons; bottom of skirt at front is also trimmed with buttons and can be worn open or closed for sports wear; colors, rose, white or sand $5.75
1784 Washable Separate Skirt, trimmed at side with the new rever patch pocket which has pearl lozenge buttons, detachable belt; bottom of skirt can be worn open, for tennis or golf wear, and is finished with buttons same as on pocket; in white cotton Bedford cord or khaki cloth $2.90
1784A Above model can be ordered in white linen, at $5.50; or in ratine, at 3.85
1785 Misses' Separate Skirt, of washable gabardine in flare model; wide detachable shaped belt, patch pockets with flaps, trimmed with large bound buttonholes and olive shaped buttons; in white or tan $6.75
1786 Washable Tailored Skirt, buttoned entirely down the front with large iridescent pearl buttons; patch pocket and detachable belt are also finished with buttons to match front; back is slightly gathered; colors, white and tan gabardine or Palm Beach cloth in natural color $4.85

1915 | 1915

DEPARTMENT FOR YOUNG GIRLS

In ordering, the measures taken from a dress or coat that fits satisfactorily, allowing for growth, will be sufficient
The sizes and colors in which the garments can be furnished are mentioned in the various descriptions

1801   Unlined Reefer, of tan covert cloth, with plain loose back and green cloth collar, patch pockets; sizes, 8 to 16 . . . . $7.85

1802   Coat, of black and white checked worsted, with wide belt of self material, button trimmed, Empire green silk sash in front; collar and cuffs of silk trimmed self material; unlined; sizes, 8 to 16 . . . . 13.50

1803   Coat, of light weight navy blue diagonal cheviot, having slightly gathered back with a wide belt, turnback cuffs and detachable white piqué collar; peau de cygne lined throughout; sizes, 6 to 16 . . . . 12.50

1804   Navy Serge Coat, with scalloped edge linen collar and cuffs, belted back and lined with twilled sateen; sizes, 6 to 10 . . . . $5.75

1805   Smart Coat, of tan covert cloth, with fancy strappings at back, with box plait from belt, which extends across front, stitched collar and cuffs; silk-lined yoke; sizes, 8 to 16 . . . . 14.75

1806   Girl's Coat, of tan pongee, with convertible collar, loose box back and black patent leather belt; sizes, 8 to 16 years 12.50

1807   Coat, of black and white checked worsted, with plain box back, plaited effect at side front and belted all around; yoke lined self material; sizes, 6 to 16 years 5.50

DEPARTMENT FOR YOUNG GIRLS—(Continued)

In ordering, the measures taken from a dress or coat that fits satisfactorily, allowing for growth, will be sufficient
The sizes and colors in which the garments can be furnished are mentioned in the various descriptions

1810 Hand-embroidered White Lingerie Dress, Russian model, with box-plaited front and back; satin ribbon girdle, daintily hand-scalloped yoke and cuffs; sizes, 6 to 12 years $3.90

1811 Fine White Voile Dress, trimmed with hand-embroidery and fine imitation Venise lace; wide satin girdle with bow at back, marking the low waistline above the finely tucked skirt; sizes, 6 to 14 years 12.75

1812 Dainty Embroidered Crêpe Frock, white with Copenhagen; high-waisted model trimmed with lace; skirt gathered to becoming yoke; 10 to 16 yrs. 14.50

1813 Dainty Rose or Copenhagen Flowered White Striped Voile Frock, with box-plaited front and back, white organdie collar and cuffs and two

narrow colored velvet ribbon belts; sizes, 6 to 12 years $5.75

1814 White Cotton Voile Dress, high-waisted model; yoke has smocking and fine imitation Venise lace; skirt tucked above hem and attached under a ribbon girdle, finished with a rosette; loose ends at back; sizes, 6 to 10 years 7.85

1815 Fine White Voile Dress, with hand-embroidery, loose bolero effect; edged with Valenciennes lace, Valenciennes insertion in waist, satin girdle with sash ends at back; sizes, 6 to 14 years 10.50

1816 White Cotton Voile Frock, in Russian style, with hand-embroidered front, collar and cuffs; two tucked box plaits front and back, and a wide satin girdle with bow at side; sizes, 6 to 12 years 5.50

1915 · 1915

DEPARTMENT FOR YOUNG GIRLS—(Continued)

In ordering, the measures taken from a dress or coat that fits satisfactorily, allowing for growth, will be
sufficient. The sizes and colors in which the garments may be furnished are mentioned in the descriptions

1820 Showerproof Coat, suitable for street or motor
wear, of the new black and white wool check,
combined with blue or gold; loose belt and
patch pockets; trimmed novelty buttons; sizes,
8 to 16 years $9.75

1821 Young Girl's Dress, of ramie linen, with fullness falling from a yoke; hand-embroidered
white collar and crochet button trimmed vestee;
circular skirt; colors, green or white; sizes, 10
to 16 years 6.75

1822 Striped Challie Dress, loose yoke over waist
which has side plaited front; white embroidery
collar and cuffs; plaited skirt; colors, green or
brown; sizes, 6 to 14 years 7.75

1823 Empire Dress, of white French linen, with rose
or Copenhagen collar, cuffs and buttons; patch
pockets on either side; sizes, 6 to 10 years . . 5.85

1824 Russian Dress, of rustique linen; collar and
cuffs trimmed with hand-embroidery; wide self
belt trimmed with pearl buttons, black tie;
oyster color or rose; sizes, 6 to 12 years . . $5.75

1825 White Linen Dress, with new jumper effect
over tucked batiste waist; hand-embroidered
pockets and pearl buttons; plaited skirt; sizes,
6 to 14 years 6.25

1826 Young Girl's Two-piece Suit, of navy blue
serge or black and white check; yoke in front
and back of coat, with fullness in front and box
plait down back; belt, collar and cuffs of self
material with white faille collar; lined with
peau de cygne; double side plait on either
side of front and back of skirt; sizes, 12 to 16
years 19.50

SMART DESIGNS FOR   THE YOUNGER SET

In ordering, the measures taken from a dress or coat that fits satisfactorily, allowing for growth, will be sufficient. The sizes and colors in which the garments may be furnished are mentioned in the descriptions

1830 Smocked Chambray Dress; side plaits serve as appropriate front and back finish; hand-embroidery adds the desired touch to collar and cuffs, and plaited skirt is always becoming to the girlish figure; colors, tan or green; sizes, 6 to 14 years $6.50

1831 Checked Gingham Bloomer Dress. in Russian style; dimity collar and cuffs; vestee effect open in front, wide self belt; colors, pink or blue; sizes, 6 to 12 years   2.35

1832 Waist Dress, of plaid gingham; dainty model with white hemstitched dimity collar, cuffs and belt, and popular double skirt effect; colors, blue or pink; sizes, 8 to 14 years 2.00

1833 Chambray Dress, two box plaits laid in at front and back, white rep collar with neat scalloped edge, crochet

button trimming, wide belt; colors, green or tan; sizes, 6 to 14 years $2.25

1834 Checked Gingham and Plain Chambray are effectively combined in this Dress, with white rep collar and cuffs and black velvet ribbon belt; colors, pink or blue; sizes, 8 to 14 years 3.25

1835 Attractive Frock, of chambray; front quaintly smocked, box plaits laid at front and back; collar and cuffs prettily hand-embroidered, and a smart little belt of self material appearing at side and back; colors, green or blue; sizes, 6 to 12 years 2.65

1836 Russian Model, of imported checked gingham, with piqué collar, cuffs and belt; front and back box-plaited; collar and cuffs attractively hand-embroidered; colors, blue or pink; sizes, 6 to 12 years 4.75

SMART DESIGNS FOR THE YOUNGER SET

In ordering, the measures taken from a dress or coat that fits satisfactorily, allowing for growth, will be sufficient. The sizes and colors in which the garments may be furnished are mentioned in the descriptions

1840 Regulation Dress, of linen, with embroidered collar and sleeves; silk tie; colors, white or Belgium blue; sizes, 10 to 16 years $6.25

1841 Detachable middy waist and plaited skirt of drill; in all white, or white combined with navy; sizes, 6 to 12 years 1.65

1842 Middy Blouse, of white drill, with navy or all white combination; sizes, 6 to 20 years 80

1843 Middy Skirt, of white or navy drill; box-plaited back and open front; sizes, 6 to 16 years 1.00

1844 New Suspender Dress, of checked gingham; exceptionally attractive; the waist consists of white lawn with dainty plaiting and velvet tie, while the plaited overskirt is attached under a wide belt of the material; colors, green or brown; sizes, 8 to 16 years $4.50

1845 Smart Dress, of striped garicord; a two piece model, with belted back and two patch pockets; a white hemstitched piqué collar contrasting prettily with the self cuffs and plain skirt; colors, blue or brown; sizes, 10 to 16 years 4.85

1846 Highly Practical Frock, with detachable Belgium blue linen pocketed skirt, which buttons to the white linen waist; finished with colored linen collar and cuffs and a jaunty silk tie; sizes, 6 to 14 years 5.50

1847 Tan Dress, of beach cloth; box-plaited front, and wide self belt, emphasized by the colored linen collar and cuffs and black silk tie; a yoke features the skirt, which is becomingly plaited at side; sizes, 10 to 16 years 7.75

THE FASSO CORSET

The Fasso embodies the art of corset designing, which means the combination of Comfort and Unquestioned Style. Created according to the French interpretation of natural line and beauty of figure, it is imported direct from Paris for the exclusive control of B. Altman & Co., and in twenty-four distinctly different styles, it solves the problem of correct corseting for every figure — from the very slender to the stoutest.

Fabrics and corresponding prices range as follows:

Plain Coutil . . . . . . $10.50 to $25.00
Tricot and Tricotine . . . 13.50 to 30.00
Batiste . . . . 13.50 to 17.50
Broché . . . . 11.75 to 22.50

Style 149 (illustrated on figure), is made of Coutil, with real whalebone, and well boned at back; suitable for medium and full figures; sizes, 19 to 30 . . . . $12.50

An extensive variety of Coutil, Linen, Serge and Tricot models, ranging in price from $7.50 to $30.00, leaves nothing unsupplied in this department's complete assortment of Imported Corsets.

The
FASSO
STYLE 149

WOVEN ELASTIC MODELS

In its many peculiar adaptations, the Elastic Support is a boon to the full figure, indispensable for equestrian or sports wear, and an excellent confinement for the uncorseted figure. The woman who appreciates the Specially Woven Elastic Support will find at all times a very extensive assortment of Corsets, Envelop-pantes, Bust Supporters and Corselets, in the following range of prices:

Elastic Corsets . . . . . $10.50 to $17.50
Enveloppantes (hip reducers) 8.50 to 12.50
Corselets . . . . 10.50 to 17.50
Bust Supporters . . . . . 7.50 to 18.50

Imported Bust Supporters, including an exceptional variety of fine Hand-embroidered and Real Lace models, are constantly maintained in stock.

Front Steels, pair, 25c. and 35c.; **Side Steels,** pair, 20c., 25c., 30c. and 35c. In ordering please mention the style of corset and length of side steels required.

Especial attention is given to all correspondence; individual requirements are carefully considered, and all corsets selected by expert corsetieres.

THE ESNAH
AND
B. A. & CO. CORSET

1901 Sizes, 19 to 36. B. A. & Co. (own make), style 63 French coutil; front steel, 12 inches; medium bust, long over hips and back, lacing below front steel; for stout figures; white $10.50

1902 Sizes, 19 to 30. B. A. & Co. (own make), style 62 French coutil or batiste; front steel, 10½ in.; medium low bust, long over hips and back, lacing below front steel; for slender and medium figures; white
$8.50

1903 Laced Front Corset, of white coutil; medium low bust, long hips and back; three pairs of hose supporters; for average figures; sizes, 20 to 30 . $3.50

The Esnah, Style 1506

1904 Sizes, 20 to 30. French coutil; low bust, very long and close-fitting hips and back; for medium figures
$15.00

1901

1902

B. A. & Co.
STYLE 62

B. A. & Co.
STYLE 63

1904

1903

Esnah
STYLE 1506

WOMEN'S CORSETS AND BRASSIÈRES

1910   Sizes, 19 to 26. Batiste Corset; front steel, 11 inches; very low bust; medium long over hips and back; band of elastic across top under arm; for slender figures; white $1.50

1911   White Coutil Redfern Corset; front steel, 9½ inches, well boned, low bust, long hips, with 3 pairs, hose supporters; for medium and stout figures; sizes, 20 to 36 . . . . $4.00

1912   Sizes, 23 to 32. Maternity Corset, coutil; length of front, 15 inches; elastic bands at front, laced on sides and in back; white . 3.00

1913   Sizes, 18 to 25. Coutil Corset "American Lady", model 236; low bust, long hips and back; for slender and average figures; white 2.00

1914   Corset, white coutil; front steel, 9½ inches; lightly boned, with elastic gore in bust; low bust and long straight hip, lacing at bottom of front steel; for slender and medium figures; sizes, 19 to 30 . . . . 3.00

1915   Sizes, 18 to 30. Coutil Corset; front steel, 10½ inches; girdle top, very long at sides; for slender and medium figures; white . . 3.50

1915A   Similar style, longer in back, cotton batiste 3.50

1915B   Sizes, 32 to 46. "Brassière Directoire", of fine muslin; open front, closed back; elastic under arm, assuring graceful poise with every movement of the figure; hooks and eyes down front; lace trimmed; white $1.00

1916   Sizes, 18 to 28. Batiste Corset; front steel, 9 inches; low bust and medium long over hips and back; for slender figures; white . $2.00

1917   Sizes, 18 to 30. Tricot Corset, girdle top, long hips; for slender and medium figures; white $5.00

1917A   Brassières, made of white cotton mesh with ribbon over shoulders; buttoned in back with elastic straps; sizes, 32 to 46 . . . . $1.00

1926 1927 1928 1929 1930 1931 1932

WOMEN'S BRASSIÈRES, CORSET WAISTS AND ACCESSORIES ALSO MISSES' AND CHILDREN'S WAISTS

1926 Brassière, made of tucked lawn, with band of linen lace imitation filet top and bottom; hooks and eyes down back; sizes, 32 to 46 . . . . $3.50

1927 Brassière, made of tape and lace; open front with hooks and eyes and laced in back; sizes, 32 to 46 . . $1.50

1928 Brassière, of silk jersey; trimmed at top with Valenciennes lace and baby ribbon, satin ribbon over shoulders, boned under arm; fastens in back with hooks and eyes; in pink and white; sizes, 32 to 44 inches $1.95

1929 Brassière, made of imitation Cluny lace with linen under arm, ribbon bows on front; hooks and eyes down back; sizes, 32 to 46 . . . . $2.50

1930 Bust Supporter, tight fitting; open front, laced at back; made of fine muslin and lace trimmed; sizes, 32 to 46 . . . . $ .50

1931 Brassière, made of fine white cotton mesh; trimmed with imitation Cluny lace; hooks and eyes down front; sizes, 32 to 46 . . . . $1.00

1932 Brassière, made of net with fine net sleeves and shields; buttons and crosses in front; sizes, 32 to 46 $ .85

1932A Equestrian Belt, suitable for golfing and all out-door sports, made of plain double batiste; extremely soft front steel; closed back with strips of elastic; two pairs of supporters; sizes, 22 to 34 . . . . $15.00

Styles Not Illustrated

1933 Sizes, 32 to 46. Bust Supporter, made of fine muslin; length at front, 5½ inches; buttoned front and laced in back; white $1.50

1934 Sizes, 32 to 46. Brassière, made of net, trimmed with embroidered edging; fine net sleeves and under arm shields; buttoned front and finished with tapes to tie around waist; white $1.00

1935 Sizes, 32 to 46. B. A. & Co. Brassière of fine net, with under arm shields; closed back, hooks and eyes down front; white $2.00

1935A Similar style, but plain finish at top; white . .   1.50

1936 Sizes, 32 to 46. "Brassière Directoire", of muslin; buttoned at front and lace trimmed $1.00

A large variety of Corset Waists for Women, $1.00 to $3.00. Misses' Waists, 50c. to $1.00. Boys' Underwaists, 35c. to 55c. Also Sachets in various shapes, 50c. to $1.50. Shirt-waist Ruffles, 45c. to 95c. Hose Supporters to sew on front of Corsets, 35c. and 50c.; of shirred ribbon, 75c. and $1.10. Hip Supporters, to sew on side of Corset, 35c. and 60c.; of shirred ribbon, $1.00 and $1.75 per pair

N. B.—Any style of Coutil Corset can be altered for nursing, with laps, for $1.00 extra

WOMEN'S COLORED PETTICOATS

Petticoats average 38 and 40 inches in length, with corresponding waistbands, as mentioned below. Where the lengths 38, 40 or 42 inches are not mentioned in the descriptions, they can be furnished in seven to ten days' time.

2001 Silk Jersey Top, colored or black with plaited flounce of self-color jersey; lengths, 38-inch front, 26-inch waist; 40-inch front, 28-inch waist $4.90

2002 White or Pink Crêpe de Chine, with lace trimmed flounce; length, 38-inch front, 30-inch waist $4.85

2003 White Satin, with box-plaited flounce, double front and back gores; lengths, 38 or 40-inch front, 32-inch waist with draw string $4.85

2004 Taffeta, black, white or colors, circular flounce edged with dainty plaited ruffle; length, 38-inch front, 26-inch waist; adjustable to 32 inches $4.50

2005 Silk Jersey Top, with plaited messaline flounce having deep underlay, in black, white or colors; lengths, 38-inch front, 30-inch waist; or 40-inch front, 32-inch waist $5.85

2005A Same as above, in all taffeta, black, white or colors; lengths, 38 or 40-inch front, 26-inch waist measure; adjustable to 32 inches . . $6.75

2006 Black Sateen, with side-plaited flounce, no underlay; lengths, 38 or 40-inch front, 26-inch waist; adjustable to 32 inches $1.20

2006A Same style, in extra size; lengths, 38 or 40-inch front, 60-inch hip, 34-inch waist; adjustable to 42 inches $1.75

2007 Black and White Striped Percale, with machine-scalloped edge and underpiece; lengths, 38 or 40-inch front, 32-inch waist with draw string . . $1.25

2007A Similar style to illustration No. 2007, in gray and white striped seersucker, no underpiece; lengths, 38 or 40-inch front, 32-inch waist with draw string $1.15

2007B Same as above, in white sateen, with underpiece; lengths, 38 or 40-inch front, 26-inch waist; adjustable to 32 inches $1.85

2007C Same as 2007B, light weight black sateen, with underpiece; lengths, 38 or 40-inch front, 26-inch waist; adjustable to 32 inches $1.65

2008 Pongee, in self color or jasper, circular flounce with two slightly gathered ruffles; lengths, 38 or 40-inch front, 26-inch waist; adjustable to 32 inches $5.75

2009 Messaline, black, white or colored space-plaited flounce with narrow plaited ruffle and deep underlay; lengths, 38 or 40-inch front, 26-inch waist; adjustable to 32 inches $5.50

2009A Similar style, with silk jersey top, messaline flounce, narrow underlay; lengths, 38 or 40-inch front, 26-inch waist; adjustable to 32 inches; fastening at left side front $3.90

2009B Similar style, in all messaline with narrow underlay; lengths, 38 or 40-inch front, 26-inch waist; adjustable to 32 inches; very special $3.75

Not Illustrated

2010 Black Feathersilk, with stitched flounce; length, 38-inch front, 32-inch waist with draw string $1.50

WOMEN'S NIGHT GOWNS

2101   Night Gown, of nainsook, open in front; three-quarter sleeves, tucks and hand feather-stitching; sizes, 14 to 16 inches $2.25

2102   Night Gown, of batiste, trimmed with Valenciennes lace and fine embroidery medallions inset with lace, ribbon drawn through eyelets; sizes, 14 to 16 inches .   4.50

2103   Night Gown, of nainsook, dainty model, combining Valenciennes lace, fine tucks and hand knots, finished with casing and ribbon; sizes, 14 to 17 inches . . .   3.90

2104   Night Gown, of nainsook, with Valenciennes lace insertion and edge; sizes, 14 to 17 inches 1.25

2104A Same as above; in extra size, 18 inches 1.50

2105   Night Gown, of nainsook, with yoke of Valenciennes lace, embroidery beading and ribbon; sizes, 14 to 16 inches 1.75

2106   Night Gown, of nainsook, with Valenciennes lace insertions, beading and ribbon; sizes, 14 to 16 inches .   1.90

2107   Night Gown, of batiste, trimmed with Valenciennes lace; sizes, 14 to 16 inches $2.65

2108   Night Gown, of cambric or muslin, durable model, with scalloped edge, tucks and hand feather-stitching; sizes, 13 to 17 inches 1.95

2108A Same as above; in extra size, 18 inches 2.25

2109   Night Gown, of batiste, top formed of joined Valenciennes lace insertions with ribbon drawn through; sizes, 14 and 16 inches 6.50

2110   Night Gown, of nainsook, with yoke of Valenciennes lace and embroidery insertions; sizes, 14 to 17 inches   1.75

2111   Night Gown, of batiste, combining Valenciennes lace, tucks and hand-embroidery; sizes, 14 to 16 inches . .   2.90

2111A Same as above; in extra size, 18 inches 3.15

2112   Night Gown, of nainsook, trimmed with embroidery and Valenciennes lace; sizes, 14 to 17 inches 1.65

2112A Same as above; in extra size, 18 inches 1.90

(Descriptions continued on following page)

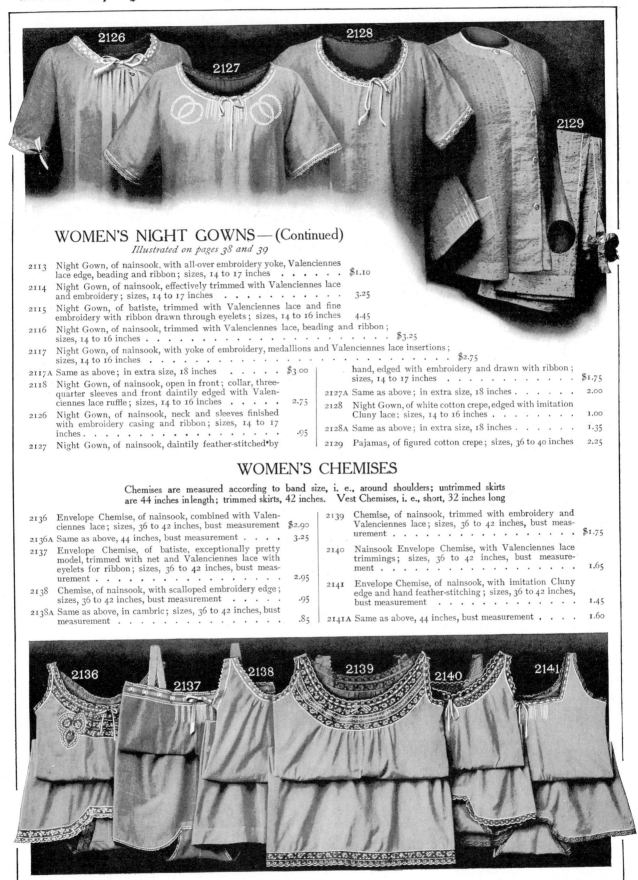

WOMEN'S NIGHT GOWNS— (Continued)
Illustrated on pages 38 and 39

2113 Night Gown, of nainsook, with all-over embroidery yoke, Valenciennes lace edge, beading and ribbon; sizes, 14 to 17 inches $1.10

2114 Night Gown, of nainsook, effectively trimmed with Valenciennes lace and embroidery; sizes, 14 to 17 inches 3.25

2115 Night Gown, of batiste, trimmed with Valenciennes lace and fine embroidery with ribbon drawn through eyelets; sizes, 14 to 16 inches 4.45

2116 Night Gown, of nainsook, trimmed with Valenciennes lace, beading and ribbon; sizes, 14 to 16 inches $3.25

2117 Night Gown, of nainsook, with yoke of embroidery, medallions and Valenciennes lace insertions; sizes, 14 to 16 inches $2.75

2117A Same as above; in extra size, 18 inches $3.00

2118 Night Gown, of nainsook, open in front; collar, three-quarter sleeves and front daintily edged with Valenciennes lace ruffle; sizes, 14 to 16 inches 2.75

2126 Night Gown, of nainsook, neck and sleeves finished with embroidery casing and ribbon; sizes, 14 to 17 inches 95

2127 Night Gown, of nainsook, daintily feather-stitched by hand, edged with embroidery and drawn with ribbon; sizes, 14 to 17 inches $1.75

2127A Same as above; in extra size, 18 inches 2.00

2128 Night Gown, of white cotton crepe, edged with imitation Cluny lace; sizes, 14 to 16 inches 1.00

2128A Same as above; in extra size, 18 inches 1.35

2129 Pajamas, of figured cotton crepe; sizes, 36 to 40 inches 2.25

WOMEN'S CHEMISES

Chemises are measured according to band size, i. e., around shoulders; untrimmed skirts are 44 inches in length; trimmed skirts, 42 inches. Vest Chemises, i. e., short, 32 inches long

2136 Envelope Chemise, of nainsook, combined with Valenciennes lace; sizes, 36 to 42 inches, bust measurement $2.90

2136A Same as above, 44 inches, bust measurement 3.25

2137 Envelope Chemise, of batiste, exceptionally pretty model, trimmed with net and Valenciennes lace with eyelets for ribbon; sizes, 36 to 42 inches, bust measurement 2.95

2138 Chemise, of nainsook, with scalloped embroidery edge; sizes, 36 to 42 inches, bust measurement 95

2138A Same as above, in cambric; sizes, 36 to 42 inches, bust measurement 85

2139 Chemise, of nainsook, trimmed with embroidery and Valenciennes lace; sizes, 36 to 42 inches, bust measurement $1.75

2140 Nainsook Envelope Chemise, with Valenciennes lace trimmings; sizes, 36 to 42 inches, bust measurement 1.65

2141 Envelope Chemise, of nainsook, with imitation Cluny edge and hand feather-stitching; sizes, 36 to 42 inches, bust measurement 1.45

2141A Same as above, 44 inches, bust measurement 1.60

WOMEN'S COMBINATION SUITS AND PRINCESS SLIPS

2150 Combination (corset cover and drawers, Poiret model), of nainsook, with ribbon bow; sizes, 36 to 42-inch bust $1.65

2151 Combination (corset cover and open or closed drawers or skirt), of nainsook, combined with dotted embroidery; sizes, 36 to 40-inch bust . 2.25

2152 Combination (corset cover and drawers), of batiste, daintily combined with footing and ribbon drawn and embroidery beading; sizes, 36 to 42-inch bust 2.85

2153 Combination (corset cover and drawers), of nainsook, with embroidery and Valenciennes lace; sizes, 36 to 42-inch bust 1.65

2154 Combination (corset cover and drawers or skirt), of nainsook, with scalloped embroidery edge; sizes, 36 to 46-inch bust 1.90

2155 Combination (corset cover and drawers or skirt), of nainsook, trimmed with Valenciennes lace and handstitching; sizes, 36 to 44-inch bust . 2.65

2156 Combination (bodice and knickerbockers), of batiste, finished with Valenciennes lace, beading and ribbon; sizes, 36 to 42-inch bust $2.90

2157 Combination (corset cover and drawers or skirt), of nainsook, trimmed with Valenciennes lace; sizes, 36 to 44-inch bust 3.25

2158 Princess Slip, of lawn, in open front style with Valenciennes lace trimming; sizes, 36 to 44-inch bust; 40-inch skirt length 4.50

2159 Princess Slip, of messaline, in white only; with double panel back and front; sizes, 36, 38 and 40-inch bust; 40-inch skirt length, $6.90; size, 44-inch bust 7.65

2160 Princess Slip, of accordion plaited crêpe de chine, in white or flesh tint, elastic at waist and top of bodice, and beautifully combined with Valenciennes lace; appropriate with lingerie and dancing frocks, or matinee; sizes, 36 to 42 inches 8.75

2161 Princess Slip, of lawn, with Valenciennes lace trimming; sizes, 36 to 44-inch bust; 38 and 42-inch skirt lengths 2.50

WOMEN'S PETTICOATS AND DRESSING SACQUES

2166 Dressing Sacque, of dotted Swiss, trimmed with Valenciennes lace ; sizes, 36 to 44 inches $1.75
2167 Dressing Sacque, of lawn, with turnover collar and cuffs of dotted embroidery ; sizes, 36 to 44 inches $1.65
2168 Dressing Sacque, of pink or blue crêpe de chine, on becoming Empire lines ; sizes, 36 to 42 inches 6.25
2169 Albatross Sacque, bound with white ribbon ; pink, blue, white 1.90
2169A Sacque, same style as above, in pink or blue crêpe de chine . 3.75
2170 Crêpe de Chine Sacque, trimmed with Valenciennes lace ; in pink, blue or lavender ; sizes, 36 to 44 inches 5.90
2170A Same as above, in figured dimity ; sizes, 36 to 46 inches . . 2.90
2171 Dainty Sacque, of hand-embroidered chiffon, lined with crêpe de chine ; colors, pink or blue 6.25
2172 Nainsook Petticoat, with double panel front and dotted embroidery ruffle, with underlay ; waist, 28 and 32 inches ; lengths, 36, 38, 40 and 42 inches 2.75
2172A Same as above, in extra size ; waist, 40 inches 3.50
2173 Petticoat, of cambric, ruffle trimmed, with imitation torchon lace and embroidery, made with underlay ; waist, 32 inches, with tape ; lengths, 36, 38, 40 and 42 inches 2.00
2173A Same as above, in extra size ; waist, 40 inches 2.75
2174 Petticoat, of nainsook, with double front panel, tambour embroidery ruffle and underlay ; waist, 28 and 34 inches, with tape ; lengths, 36, 38, 40 and 42 inches 3.65
2175 Nainsook Petticoat, double panel front, full circular flounce of Valenciennes lace and embroidery, with underlay ; waist, 32 inches, with tape ; lengths, 36, 38, 40 and 42 inches . . . 5.85
2175A Same as above, in extra size ; waist, 40 inches 7.25
2176 Cambric Petticoat, having eyelet embroidery ruffle, with underlay ; waist, 28 and 32 inches ; lengths, 36, 38, 40 and 42 inches 2.90
2176A Same as above, in extra size ; waist, 40 inches 3.65
2177 Sateen Petticoat, cut on new lines, with machine-scalloped edge; waist, 28 and 32 in., with tape; lengths, 36, 38, 40 and 42 in. 1.50
2177A Same as above, in extra size ; waist, 40 inches 1.85
2178 Nainsook Petticoat, with double front panel, flounce of Valenciennes lace and embroidery, with underlay ; waist, 28 and 32 inches ; lengths, 36, 38, 40 and 42 inches 2.90
2178A Same as above, in extra size ; waist, 40 inches 4.00
2179 Petticoat, of cambric, attractive flounce trimmed with Valenciennes lace and embroidery, made with underlay ; waist, 32 inches, with tape ; lengths, 36, 38, 40 and 42 inches . . . 2.50
2180 Cambric Petticoat, for golf or tennis, ruffle of tambour embroidery, without underlay ; waist, 32 inches, with tape ; lengths, 36, 38 and 40 inches 1.25
2181 Nainsook Petticoat, an elaborate model, with double panel front and full flounce trimmed with Valenciennes lace and embroidery, with underlay ; waist, 28 and 34 inches ; lengths, 36, 38, 40 and 42 inches 8.75
2182 Petticoat, of cambric, with dotted embroidery ruffle and underlay ; waist, 28 and 32 inches ; lengths, 36, 38, 40 and 42 inches 1.50
2182A Same as above, in extra size ; waist, 36 and 40 inches . . . 2.00

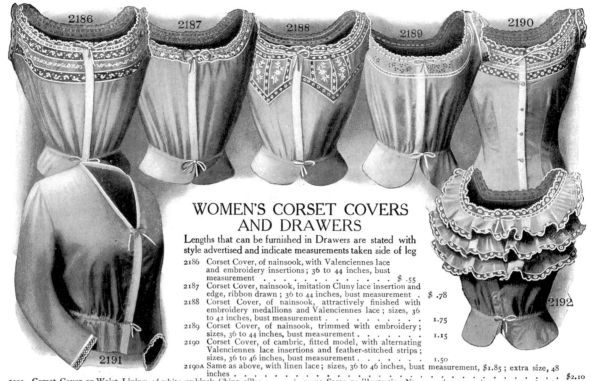

WOMEN'S CORSET COVERS AND DRAWERS

Lengths that can be furnished in Drawers are stated with
style advertised and indicate measurements taken side of leg

2186 Corset Cover, of nainsook, with Valenciennes lace
and embroidery insertions; 36 to 44 inches, bust
measurement . . . . $ .55
2187 Corset Cover, nainsook, imitation Cluny lace insertion and
edge, ribbon drawn ; 36 to 44 inches, bust measurement . $ .78
2188 Corset Cover, of nainsook, attractively finished with
embroidery medallions and Valenciennes lace ; sizes, 36
to 42 inches, bust measurement 1.75
2189 Corset Cover, of nainsook, trimmed with embroidery ;
sizes, 36 to 44 inches, bust measurement 1.15
2190 Corset Cover, of cambric, fitted model, with alternating
Valenciennes lace insertions and feather-stitched strips ;
sizes, 36 to 46 inches, bust measurement 1.50
2190A Same as above, with linen lace ; sizes, 36 to 46 inches, bust measurement, $1.85 ; extra size, 48
inches . . . .

2191 Corset Cover or Waist Lining, of white or black China silk ;
sizes, 36 to 44 inches, bust measurement $3.50
2191A Same as above, in low neck and short sleeve style 2.75
2192 Corset Cover, nainsook, with three lawn ruffles, edged with
Valenciennes lace ; sizes, 34 to 40 inches, bust measurement . 1.50
2193 Drawers, of nainsook, trimmed with tambour embroidery ;
open or closed ; lengths, 23 and 25 inches. 1.15
2193A Same as above; extra size; open only; lengths, 23 and 25 inches 1.30
2194 Knickerbocker Drawers, of nainsook, Valenciennes lace points;
open or closed ; length, 25 inches 2.95
2195 Drawers, of nainsook, attractive design, with lace and dotted
embroidery insertions; open or closed ; lengths, 21, 23 and 25 in. 1.65
2195A Same as above, in extra size; open or closed ; lengths, 23 and
25 inches 1.85
2196 Nainsook Drawers, with scalloped embroidery edge and seam
veining; open or closed ; lengths, 21, 23 and 25 inches . . 1.10
2197 Cambric Drawers, with embroidery ruffle; open or closed ;
lengths, 23, 25 and 27 inches 1.35

2197A Same as illustration No. 2197, in extra size; open or closed ;
lengths, 23, 25 and 27 inches $2.10
2197B Same style as illustration No. 2197, in double extra size ; open
only ; lengths, 23, 25 and 27 inches 1.50
2197C Drawers, same as illustration No. 2197, in triple extra size;
open only ; lengths, 25 and 27 inches 1.65
2198 Drawers, of nainsook, embroidery trimmed ; open or closed ;
lengths, 23 and 25 inches 1.80
2198A Same as above, in extra size; open or closed ; lengths, 23 and
25 inches 1.45
2199 Nainsook Drawers, in circular style, fitted at waistband and
trimmed with tambour embroidery ; open only ; lengths,
21, 23 and 25 inches 1.55
2200 Cambric Drawers, trimmed with embroidery; open or closed ;
lengths, 23, 25 and 27 inches 1.65
2200A Same as above, in extra size; open or closed ; lengths, 23, 25
and 27 inches 55
2201 Drawers, of nainsook, ruffle with Valenciennes lace; open
only ; lengths, 21 and 23 inches 65
                                                         1.35

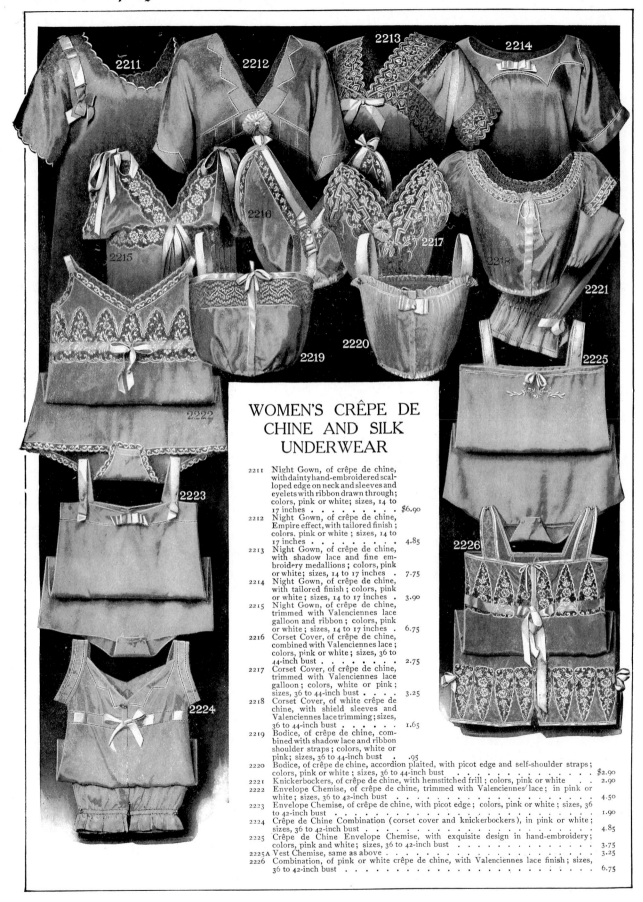

WOMEN'S CRÊPE DE CHINE AND SILK UNDERWEAR

2211 Night Gown, of crêpe de chine, with dainty hand-embroidered scalloped edge on neck and sleeves and eyelets with ribbon drawn through; colors, pink or white; sizes, 14 to 17 inches $6.90

2212 Night Gown, of crêpe de chine, Empire effect, with tailored finish; colors. pink or white; sizes, 14 to 17 inches 4.85

2213 Night Gown, of crêpe de chine, with shadow lace and fine embroidery medallions; colors, pink or white; sizes, 14 to 17 inches . 7.75

2214 Night Gown, of crêpe de chine, with tailored finish; colors, pink or white; sizes, 14 to 17 inches . 3.90

2215 Night Gown, of crêpe de chine, trimmed with Valenciennes lace galloon and ribbon; colors, pink or white; sizes, 14 to 17 inches . 6.75

2216 Corset Cover, of crêpe de chine, combined with Valenciennes lace; colors, pink or white; sizes, 36 to 44-inch bust 2.75

2217 Corset Cover, of crêpe de chine, trimmed with Valenciennes lace galloon; colors, white or pink; sizes, 36 to 44-inch bust 3.25

2218 Corset Cover, of white crêpe de chine, with shield sleeves and Valenciennes lace trimming; sizes, 36 to 44-inch bust 1.65

2219 Bodice, of crêpe de chine, combined with shadow lace and ribbon shoulder straps; colors, white or pink; sizes, 36 to 44-inch bust . .95

2220 Bodice, of crêpe de chine, accordion plaited, with picot edge and self-shoulder straps; colors, pink or white; sizes, 36 to 44-inch bust $2.90

2221 Knickerbockers, of crêpe de chine, with hemstitched frill; colors, pink or white . . . 2.90

2222 Envelope Chemise, of crêpe de chine, trimmed with Valenciennes/lace; in pink or white; sizes, 36 to 42-inch bust 4.50

2223 Envelope Chemise, of crêpe de chine, with picot edge; colors, pink or white; sizes, 36 to 42-inch bust 1.90

2224 Crêpe de Chine Combination (corset cover and knickerbockers), in pink or white; sizes, 36 to 42-inch bust 4.85

2225 Crêpe de Chine Envelope Chemise, with exquisite design in hand-embroidery; colors, pink and white; sizes, 36 to 42-inch bust 3.75

2225A Vest Chemise, same as above 3.25

2226 Combination, of pink or white crêpe de chine, with Valenciennes lace finish; sizes, 36 to 42-inch bust 6.75

FRENCH UNDERWEAR
MADE ENTIRELY BY HAND

In addition to the Hand-made French Underwear shown, single garments or entire sets for Brides' Trousseaux appropriately matched can be furnished at moderate prices. The newest conceptions in Initials, Monograms or Crests embroidered to order. Descriptions of many other more elaborately embroidered or lace-trimmed styles, not illustrated, will be sent upon request, giving detailed information as to requirements. Should any garment be temporarily out of stock, another equally desirable model will be substituted, unless otherwise instructed.

2301 Chemise, nainsook, unlaundered; sizes, 40, 42, 44 and 46 . . . . $1.35

2302 Night Gown, nainsook, insertion and edge of imitation Val., laundered; sizes, 14, 15 and 16   3.50

2303 Chemise, nainsook, insertion and edge of imitation Val., laundered; sizes, 40, 42 and 44   2.00

2304 Chemise, nainsook, unlaundered; sizes, 40, 42 and 44 . . . . 1.25

2305 Corset Cover, nainsook, insertion and edge of imitation Val., laundered; sizes, 36, 38 and 40   2.00

2306 Night Gown, nainsook, laundered; sizes, 14, 15 and 16 . . . . 2.95

2307 Envelope Chemise, nainsook, insertion and edge of imitation Val., laundered; sizes, 40, 42 and 44 . . . . 2.50

2308 Night Gown, nainsook, laundered; sizes, 14, 15 and 16 . . . . 3.90

2309 Night Gown, nainsook, laundered; sizes, 14, 15 and 16 . . . . 4.50

2310 Combination, nainsook, insertion and edge of imitation Val., laundered; sizes, 36, 38 and 40   3.75

2311 Combination, nainsook, unlaundered; sizes, 36, 38, 40 and 42 . . . . 2.95

2312 Drawers, nainsook, insertion and edge of imitation Val., laundered; lengths, 23 and 25 . . . . 2.10

2313 Drawers, nainsook, unlaundered; lengths, 23 and 25 . . . . 1.38

DRESS FABRICS FOR SPRING AND SUMMER

New Textures in Silk, Cotton and Wool at Moderate Prices

Silks of Every Hue—Exclusive Novelties in black and all colors are featured in exceptional variety; the charm of this season's silks being the new shades originated and introduced by B. Altman & Co., including Palm Beach, Delaware Peach, Arizona Silver, Oregon Green, Tuxedo Brown, Rocky Mountain Blue, Newport Tan, Gettysburg Gray and Piping Rock.

Cotton and Linen Novelties—Extremes have met this season in the clinging Voiles and sheer, stiff Organdies, embodying embroidered and beaded designs in Voiles and embroidered Organdies. Lace Cloths contribute a new plain or embroidered web mesh; Bordered Materials inspire renewed favor in deep embroidered effects; and Handkerchief Linen varies its narrow or bold wide stripes with old block prints of past fashion decades.

New Colors and Weaves in Woolen Fabrics—Navy Blue Serge shares Spring favor with Mixtures, Checked and Striped effects; New Colors of Congo Blue, French Gray, Tan or Sand as well as Palm Beach, Delaware Peach, Arizona Silver, Oregon Green, Tuxedo Brown, Rocky Mountain Blue, Newport Tan, Gettysburg Gray and Piping Rock; Seasonable Gabardines, French Serges, Faille de Laines, Plain and Printed Voiles, Etc. Motor and Sports Coatings are featured in large variety.

For out-of-town patrons two desirable qualities of serge are offered. Samples upon request.

Black, Navy or White, fifty inches wide, 85c.; Black or Navy, fifty-four inches wide, $1.10

Black and White Check, in three sizes of checks; forty-eight inches wide, $1.10

All-Silk and Silk-and-Wool Mourning Veils, also French and English Crapes for Veils and Trimmings are shown in extensive variety.

With the exception of the Bordered Fabrics, samples of any materials will be sent upon request. In writing, the colors and approximate price should be mentioned; also the style of garment for which samples are requested.

CREAM WHITE EMBROIDERED SKIRTING FLANNELS

 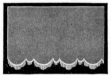 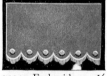  

2401 Embroidery, ½ in. deep, yard . 95c.

2402 Embroidery, ½ in. deep, yard . 48c.

2403 Embroidery, ⅜ in. deep, yard . 90c.

2404 Embroidery, ½ in. deep, yard . 95c.

2405 Embroidery, ⅝ in. deep, yard . 95c.

   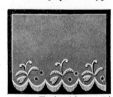 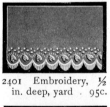

2406 Embroidery, 1⅛ in. deep, yard . 85c.

2407 Silk Warp, 1⅝ in. deep, yard $2.25

2408 Embroidery, 1⅝ in. deep, yard $1.25

2409 Embroidery, ⅞ in. deep, yard . 60c.

2410 Embroidery, 1 in. deep, yard . 90c.

2411 Embroidery, 2⅛ in. deep, yard $1.65

2412 Twilled Unshrinkable, embroidered. 1 in. deep, yard . $1.10

2413 Embroidery, 1⅝ in. deep, yard . 8cc.

2414 Twilled Unshrinkable, embroidered, 1½ in. deep, yard, $1.50

2415 Hemstitched Embroidery, 2⅜ in. deep, yard . . . $1.15

2416 Plain Scallop (*not illustrated*), yard . . . $ .48   2417 Plain Scallop and Dot (*not illustrated*), yard $ .50

2501
2502
2503
2508
2504
2507
2522
3126
3127
2505
2506
2523
2524
2525
3128
2509
2516
2515
2513
2511
2512
2517
2519
2520
2521
2518
2514
2510

MISSES' AND CHILDREN'S UNDERWEAR

With Practical Rompers for Little Folk

Measurements given for Gowns are the lengths from front of neck. Lengths for Drawers are the measurements from underneath band

2526　　2527

2530

2529

2528

2501 Gown, of nainsook, with kimono sleeves; neatly finished with machine-hemstitched bias folds; lengths, 28, 32 and 37 inches, 75c.; 42, 45, 46 and 52 inches . . . . . $ .95
2502 Gown, of cambric, trimmed with embroidery insertion and edge; lengths, 46 and 52 inches 1.35
2503 Gown, of nainsook, in Empire style; dainty combination of lace embroidery and ribbon; length, 52 inches 2.25
2504 Gown, of durable cambric, trimmed with embroidery and ribbon; lengths, 46 and 52 inches 1.10
2505 Gown, of nainsook, lace and ribbon trimmed; lengths, 46 and 52 inches 1.45
2506 Nainsook Gown, in Empire style; trimmed with lace, embroidery and ribbon; length, 52 inches . 1.85
2507 Corset Cover, nainsook, lace and ribbon trimmed; 34 and 36 in.(bust) .68
2508 **Dainty Bodice, of white crepe de chine, lace and ribbon trimmed; size, 36 inches; special value . . .** 1.35
2509 Corset Cover, of nainsook, embroidery and ribbon trimmed; sizes, 34 and 36 inches (bust) 75
2510 Nainsook Corset Cover, trimmed with heavy cotton lace, briar stitching and tucks; sizes, 34 and 36 inches (bust) 90
2511 Nainsook Combination, corset cover and closed drawers, with lace and embroidery trimming; size, 16 years 1.65
2512 Princess Slip, of nainsook, trimmed with Valenciennes lace, and ribbon drawn; sizes, 14 and 16 years 3 75
2513 Nainsook Princess Slip, embroidery trimmed; sizes, 6 and 8 years, $1.50; 10 and 12 years, $1.75; 14 and 16 years . . . 1.85
2514 Child's Princess Slip, lawn, Valenciennes lace and embroidery trimmed, buttoning on shoulder; sizes, 6 years, $1.90; 8 years, $2.00; 10 and 12 years 2.25
2515 Skirt, of nainsook, with dainty flounce of tucks and lace, and lace-trimmed dust ruffle; length, 36 inches 1.85
2516 Skirt, of nainsook, dotted embroidery ruffle and ribbon beading; lengths, 16, 20, 24, 28, 32 and 36 inches 1.50
2517 Skirt, of cambric, with embroidery ruffle; lengths, 16, 20, 24, 28, 32, 34 and 36 inches 1.00
2518 Skirt, of cambric, with embroidery flounce and dust ruffle; lengths, 34 and 36 inches 1.50
2519 Double V-waists, no cords, for boys and girls; sizes, 4 to 12 years .50
2519A Infants' sizes, 2 to 3 years 40
2520 Cambric Full Waist, neck and armholes edged with lace, two rows of tape buttons for underwear; sizes, 4 to 14 years 50
2521 Muslin Night Drawers as follows:

SIZE	LENGTH INCHES	AGE YEARS	WITHOUT TRIMMING	EDGE ON NECK AND SLEEVES
1	30	2 and 3	$ .60	$ .70
2	34	4 and 5	.65	.80
3	38	6 and 7	.75	.90
4	42	8 and 9	.85	.95
5	46	10 and 12	.95	1.00

2522 Drawers, of muslin, tucks and embroidery; lengths, 9 inches, 45c.; 10 inches, 47c.; 12 inches, 50c.; 14 inches, 53c.; 16 inches, 57c.; 18 inches, 60c.; 20 inches, 62c.; 22 inches, 65c.; 25 inches $ .68
2523 Drawers, of muslin, hem and tucks; length, 9 inches, 25c.; 10 inches, 30c.; 12 inches, 30c.; 14 inches, 35c.; 16 inches, 40c.; 18 inches, 40c.; 20 inches, 45c.; 22 inches, 45c.; 25 inches . . .50
2524 Drawers, of nainsook, with hemstitched hem and embroidery ruffle; lengths, 20 and 22 inches 75
2525 Drawers, of nainsook, combined with lace and embroidery; length, 22 inches 95
2526 Rompers, of seersucker, in white, blue or pink stripe; neck and sleeves neatly finished with machine-scalloped edge; sizes, 1 to 3 years 50
2527 Rompers, of white seersucker, with light blue trimming; sizes, 2 to 5 years 75
2528 Rompers, with white cambric waist, with blue or tan crash trousers; sizes, 2 to 6 years 55
2529 Rompers, of white cambric, blue trimming; sizes, 2 to 4 years .55
2530 Rompers, of cadet or tan chambray, piped with white; sizes, 2 to 6 years 95
2531 Rompers, of blue chambray, with collar and cuffs of white hemstitched poplin; practical model; sizes, 1 to 3 years . . . 1.35

TRADE MARK
B. A. & CO.

MISSES' AND CHILDREN'S KNITTED UNDERWEAR

Knitted Undergarments, described as Nos. 3134 to 3139 are made exclusively for B. Altman & Co. in fine Cotton Gauze, also Gauze Merino (wool and cotton) in specially selected styles, particularly well finished

In ordering Vests, please state whether high neck and long sleeves, high neck and short sleeves or low neck is desired; Pantalets are open at sides; age may be given when size is not known.

	SIZES:	18	20	22	24	26	28	30	32	34
3126	Cotton Union Suits, knee length, as illustrated on page 46		$ .75	$ .75	$ .75	$ .75	$ .75	$ .75	$ .75	
3127	Ribbed Cotton Vests, as illustrated on page 46			.30	.30	.30	.30	.40	.40	$.40
3128	Cotton Union Suits, short trunk style, as illustrated on page 46	$ .50	.50	.50	.50	.50	.50	.50		
3129	Cotton Gauze Vests, high neck and long sleeves		.25	.25	.25	.35	.35	.35	.35	
3130	Cotton Gauze Vests, high neck and short sleeves, or low neck and sleeveless style . .		.25	.25	.25	.35	.35	.35	.35	.35
3131	Cotton Gauze Pantalets, same quality as Nos. 3129 and 3130; short trunk style (above knee)		.25	.25	.25	.35	.35	.35	.35	
3132	Gauze Merino (cotton and wool) Vests, high or low neck and short sleeves		.60	.65	.70	.75	.80	.85	.90	
3133	Gauze Merino (cotton and wool) Pantalets, knee length, also short trunk style	.60	.65	.70	.75	.80	.85	.90		
3134	B. Altman & Co. Brand (Betalph), Fine Cotton Gauze Vests, low neck no sleeves . .	.60	.65	.70	.75	.80	.85	.90	.95	1.00
3135	Pantalets, same quality as No. 3134, short trunk style	.65	.70	.75	.80	.85	.90	.95		
3136	B. Altman & Co. Brand (Betalph) Fine Quality Gauze Merino (wool and cotton) Vests, full fashioned, high neck and short sleeves or low neck and no sleeves	.90	1.00	1.10	1.20	1.30	1.40	1.50	1.60	1.70
3137	Pantalets, same quality as No. 3136, knee length, also short trunk style	1.00	1.10	1.20	1.30	1.40	1.50	1.60		
3138	B. Altman & Co. Brand (Betalph) Extra Fine Gauze Merino (wool and cotton) Vests, full fashioned, low neck, no sleeves			1.30	1.40	1 50	1.60	1.70	1.80	1.90	2.00
3139	Pantalets, same quality as No. 3138, knee length	1.30	1.40	1.50	1.60	1.70	1.80	1.90		

APRONS AND CAPS

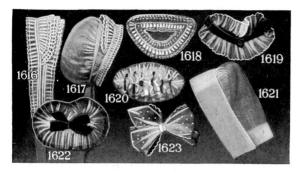

1616 Maid's Lawn Cap, ruffles lace trimmed . . . . $ .20
1617 Nurse's Cap, of lawn, ruffles lace trimmed 25
1618 Cap, of lawn, ruffles lace trimmed 05
1619 Maid's Cap, of dainty tambour, emb. and black satin ribbon .23
1620 Maid's Cap, of net, black velvet ribbon loops 18
1621 Nurse's Cap, of organdie 22
1622 Net Cap, in attractive design, with black velvet bow . . .28
1623 Dotted Swiss Bow, edged with Valenciennes lace 10
1624 Maid's Lawn Apron, bib and shoulder straps, emb. trimmed .75
1625 Dainty Lawn Apron, trimmed with effective embroidery . 1.35
1626 Nurse's Lawn Apron, attractive shoulder pieces emb. trim. .50
1627 Maid's Lawn Apron 85
1627A Nurse's Apron, cambric, gored skirt and bib, same shape as
       No. 1627, with tie strings or with button and buttonhole on band .85
1628 Net Apron, with collar and cuffs to match 95
1628A Similar style, in lawn 75
1629 Maid's Lawn Apron, bib and strap edged with scallop. emb. .50
1630 Sewing Apron, of lawn, with two pockets, edged with
       durable ric-rac braid 25
1631 Dotted Swiss Apron, prettily ruffled and finished with
       hemstitching 50

Aprons—Not Illustrated

1632   Muslin Apron, extra wide band with button and buttonhole $ .50
1632A Same style as above, with bib and shoulder straps 75
1633   Butler's Apron, of white cotton duck, 40c.; or of checked
        gingham 60
1634   Apron, princess style, of blue checked gingham 50
1635   Cover-all Apron, with cap to match ; in blue and white or
        pink and white percale, 75c., $1.00 and 1.10

MISSES' COLORED PETTICOATS

Silk Petticoats for Misses can be supplied in 14, 16 and 18-year sizes. Those carried in stock average about 26 inches, waist measure, and 36 inches long — the styles not quoted in 34-inch lengths can be ordered, requiring about one week to furnish

2551 All-silk Jersey Skirt, with jersey silk French plaited flounce;
       in white, colors or black ; length, 36 inches $4.90
2552 White Crêpe de Chine Skirt, circular flounce edged with lace
       ruffle and inset with lace medallions ; plaited dust ruffle of
       crêpe de chine; length, 36 inches 5.75
2553 Soft Finish Sateen Skirt, with accordion plaited flounce ; in
       blue, gray or black ; length, 36 inches 1.65
2554 Skirt, of soft finish taffeta, with tucked ruffle and underlay ;
       in range of popular shades and black ; length, 36 inches . 5.75
2555 Black and White Striped Percale Skirt, tucked ruffle ; 36 inches 1.00
2556 Silk Jersey Top Skirt, with effective flounce of plaited
       messaline and dust underlay, in black and appropriate colors ;
       lengths, 34 and 36 inches 4.25
2557 Messaline Skirt, with deep flounce of fancy plaited messaline
       and dust ruffle ; in colors and black ; length, 36 inches . . . 2.90
2558 Silk Jersey Top Skirt, with plaited messaline flounce ; in
       prevailing colors and black ; length, 36 inches 2.90
2559 Skirt, of black and white striped messaline ; bias sectional
       flounce with black ruche edging and underlay of striped
       messaline ; length, 36 inches 5.50

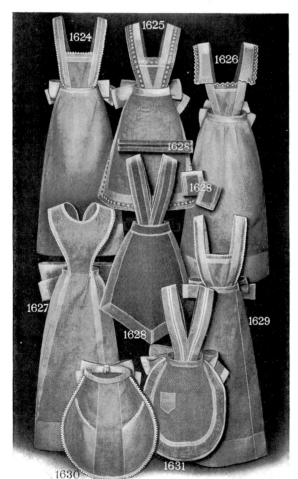

INFANTS' MISCELLANEOUS GOODS

2601 Baby's Record Book, blue or pink decorations $1.25
2602 Satin Ribbon Coat Hanger, blue or pink . . .85
2602A Similar styles, hand-painted decorations, 50c. and 1.00
2603 Rosettes, of satin ribbon; white, blue or pink .25
2604 Rosettes, of satin baby ribbon; white, blue or pink .15
2605 Clothes Hanger, hand-painted blue or pink . .75
2606 Rattle of Celluloid, hand-painted decorations in blue or pink 50
2607 Armlets, of shirred satin ribbon with hand-painted bows, in white, blue or pink 35
2608 Talcum Box, of celluloid, white, with either blue or pink hand-painted decorations . . 1.00
2609 Celluloid Set, white, with blue or pink hand-painted decorations 1.25
2609A Celluloid Set, similar to above, finer quality . 2.50
2609B Similar Set, with a rattle added 3.25
2609C Celluloid Set, consisting of comb and brush, blue or pink decorations (not illustrated) 50
2610 White Enameled Wicker Crib; 20 x 42 in.; detachable canopy stick; curtain of organdie, lace and ribbon trimmed; blue or pink China silk lined 38.00
2610A Same style as illustration, untrimmed . . . 16.50
2610B Same style, without the canopy stick . . 14.50
2610C Mattress for No. 2610, white hair, covered with white sateen 6.50
2611 Egyptian Basket, on stand, blue or pink China silk lined, organdie lace and ribbon trim; 26x14½ in. 21.00
2612 White Enameled Crib, drop sides; 28 x 52 in. 10.50
2612A Mattress, best quality South American hair, to fit crib, covered with pink or blue art ticking . 11.50
2612B China Silk Tufted Shields, for baby's crib, blue or pink 18.50
2613 Reed Nursery Chair, white enameled, lined with cretonne white ground, blue or pink flowers 8.00
2613A Same style, without tufted pads 5.25
2614 Wardrobe Hamper, white enam. with folding drawers, trimmed Swiss, Val. lace and ribbon bows, blue or pink, lower drawers with silk tufted pads 24.00
2614A Wardrobe Hamper, same as above, with blue or pink ribbon bow on cover, untrimmed $8.25

2615 Baby's Rack, white enameled frame, decorated with blue or pink figured cretonne; rubber lined pockets for toilet articles $3.25
2616 White Enameled Wicker Hamper. . . . 6.00
2616A Same as above, without bow 4.50
2617 Reed Nursery Chair, shellaced, size of opening in seat, 5½ in.; height from floor to seat, 8½ in. 2.75
2617A Same, in white enamel 4.00
2618 Toilet Set, consisting of basin, pitcher, powder box and soap dish; in ivory and gold, blue and gold, or pink and gold china; on a white enameled stand 9.50
2618A Same, with round basin; colors as above . . . 9.25
2619 Rubber Portable Bath Tub, with towel rack, faucet at bottom, pockets trimmed blue or pink ribbon; inside length, 32 in.; width, 18 in.; depth, 11 in. 11.75
2619A Similar style, 1 in. smaller throughout, plain light color wooden frame, without pockets or towel rack 7.50
2620 Fancy Straw Basket, white enameled; blue or pink silk trimming 5.75
2621 Weighing Scale, white enameled detachable basket, silk pad and bow of blue or pink ribbon . 7.75
2621A Same, with head-rest, pad and ribbon bow . . 9.75
2621B Weighing Scale and Basket, untrimmed . . 5.50
2622 White Enameled Crib, on stand, hood with flowered net, lining of China silk, blue or pink . 35.00
2622A Same, untrimmed; size at bottom, 12 x 29 inches 13.75
2622B White Hair Mattress, covered with white sateen 4.50
2623 Clothes Tree, white enameled wood, blue or pink bow, $1.95; same, hand-painted decorations 2.75

Not Illustrated

2624 Untrimmed Wicker Basket; size, 12 x 16 . $ .50
2625 Palm Leaf Hamper; length, 24 inches; width, 16 inches; depth, 12 inches 6.25
2626 Similar style, trimmed in organdie and lace with blue or pink ribbon bow, lined blue or pink silesia 19.75
2627 Eureka Bed Clothes Fasteners, white cotton, 25c.; silk 35

INFANTS' MISCELLANEOUS GOODS

2630 **Hand-made Percale Pillow Case**; size, 12 x 16 inches; with hand-embroidered scallop and dot $1.00
2631 **Hand-made, Hand-embroidered Nainsook Pillow Case**; size, 12 x 16 inches 3.00
2632 **Cream Knit Worsted Afghan**, with cream, blue or pink border; size, 30 x 35 inches 3.50
2632A **Cream Wrapping Blanket**, crocheted worsted, with cream, blue or pink border; size, 36 x 36 inches 2.35
2633 **Nainsook Afghan**, trimmed with embroidery 2.00
2633A **White Corduroy Afghan**, China silk lined and interlined 2.65
2634 **Cream Knit Sweater**, all wool, with white, blue or pink border; sizes, 1 to 3 years 1.10
2634A **Similar style**, without fancy knit border down front; sizes and colors as above 1.50
2634B **Another style**, with band and ribbon at neck instead of turn-back collar; colors as above ; infant's size to 2 years . . 1.45
2635 **Knit Sweater**, all wool; sizes, 1½ to 4 years ; white or Copenhagen 1.50
2636 **Flannel Skirt**, hand-embroidered scallop 1.95
2636A **Other styles**, finer flannel, $3.90 . . . . 4.50
2636B **Similar shape Skirt, with a Nainsook Waist**, button on shoulder, $1.95, $3.25 . . . . 3.75
2636C **Same as above**, with hem, hand feather-stitched 1.75
2637 **Infant's Cream Cashmere Wrapper**, with hand-embroidered scallop and dot, embroidered in white, blue or pink . . 2.90
2637A **Other styles**, hand-embroidered, with China silk lining; $6.00, $7.50 . . . . . . 8.00
2637B **Cream Cashmere Wrapper**, collar, cuffs and down front of wrapper hand-crochet stitched, in white, blue or pink . . 2.75
2637C **Cream Flannel Wrapper**, collarless, stitched in white, blue or pink 1.85
2637D **Infant's Wrapper**, of flannelette, in all white, blue and white or pink and white stripe 50
2638 **Worsted Bootees**, hand-knit; white, white and blue or white and pink 40
2639 **Worsted Bootees**, hand-knit; white, white and blue or white and pink 50
2639A **Similar style**, finer 70
2639B **Silk Bootees**; white, white and blue or white and pink, $1.00 1 25
2640 **Worsted Bootees**; white, white and blue or white and pink .25
2640A **Similar style**, colors as above 20
2641 **Infants' Soft-soled Shoes**, buttoned; white, blue, pink, tan or black kid ; sizes, 1, 2 or 3 50
2642 **Soft-soled Ankle Ties**; white, blue, pink, tan or black kid; sizes, 1, 2 or 3 50
2643 **White Kid Moccasins**; white, blue or pink ribbon, also tan kid ; infant's size to 6 months only 50
2644 **White Pique Slippers**, with hand-embroidery; sizes, infant's to 6 months 1.25
2644A **Same style**, without embroidery 75
2645 **Bathing Suit**, of wool jersey knit ; colors, gray or navy blue ; sizes, 2 to 4 years 1.50

Not Illustrated

2646 **Afghan**, of white cheese cloth; tufted with white, blue or pink worsted $1.05
2647 **Bath Blanket**, of double-faced white eiderdown ; bound with white, blue or pink satin ribbon 1.95
2648 **Flannel Bands**, pinked 15
2649 **Flannel Barrow Coat**, with cambric band 50
2650 **Flannel Barrow Coat**, machine silk stitching, cambric band .75
2651 **Same style as No. 2650**, feather-stitched 1.00
2652 **Flannel Shawls**, square, with cream silk binding 90
2653 **Same style as No. 2652**, with hand-embroidered scallop . 1.65
2654 **Quilted Lap Pad**; size, 17 x 17 inches 35
2655 **Machine Quilted Pads**; size, 17 x 18 inches .20
2656 **Same style as No. 2655**; size, 27 x 40 inches 47
2657 **Bath Apron**, of Turkish toweling 1.65
2658 **Bath Apron**, of cotton stockinet 90
2659 **Cotton Diapers**, hemmed, per set of 12 pieces each : size, 18 inches, 60c. ; 22 inches, $1.00; 24 inches 1.12
2660 **Stockinet Rubber Diapers**; infant's size to 1 year 45
2661 **Cupid Diapers**, same sizes as above 55
2661A **Rubber Diapers**, sizes as above 25
2662 **White Coat Linings**, sateen with Canton flannel interlining; sizes, 6 months to 4 years 1.50
2663 **Same style as No. 2662**, of China silk, tufted, interlined with cotton wadding 4.00
2664 **Lawn Pillow Case**; 14 x 18 inches ; machine-hemstitched ruffle .60
2665 **Lawn Pillow Case**; with tucks and ruffle of embroidery ; 14 x 18 inches 75
2666 **Lawn Pillow Case**; 14 x 18 in. ; machine-hemstitched hem .40
2667 **Pillow Case**, of linen, machine-stitched hem 75
2668 **Cotton Crib Sheets**, with machine-stitched hem, each . . .45
2669 **Cotton Crib Sheets**, with machine-hemstitched hems, each .75
2669A **Same**, finer, with hand-hemstitched hems, each 1.25
2669B **Same**, with hand-hemmed hem, each 95
2670 **Infants' Pillows**; size, 14 x 18 inches ; muslin, filled with down, each, 70c. and 90
2671 **Same style as above**, of sateen, filled with hair, each . . 1.00

INFANTS' MISCELLANEOUS GOODS   (Continued)

2672   **Hood Shawl,** of cream cashmere, with cream, blue or pink hand-embroidery, lined with silk $3.50
2672A   **Hood Shawl,** of cream cashmere, with cream, blue or pink hand-embroidered scallop, unlined 2.75
2673   **Silk and Wool Bands;** sizes, 3 months to 2 years, 55c.; extra size, to fit up to 4 years 75
2673A   **All-wool Bands;** sizes, 3 months, 40c.; 6 months, 45c.; 9 months to 2 years, 50c.; extra size, to fit up to 4 years 60
2673B   **Cotton and Wool Bands;** sizes, 3 months to 3 years 25
2674   **Wooden Frame,** for drying infants' shirts to prevent shrinking; infant's size to 2 years 38
2675   **Bib,** of piqué, hand-embroidered scallop 25
2675A   **Feeding Bib,** of Turkish toweling 18
2675B   **Same as above,** of huckaback 30
2675C   **Feeding Bib,** of linen momie cloth, with absorbing pad 25
2676   **Hand-embroidered Bib,** of nainsook 65
2677   **Silk and Wool Shirts;** sizes, 3 months, 85c.; 6 months, 90c; 9 months, 95c.; 1 year, $1.05; 1½ years, $1.15; 2 years, $1.25; 3 to 4 years 1.40
2677A   **Cotton and Wool Shirts;** sizes, 3 months. 45c.; 6 months, 50c.; 9 months, 55c.; 1 year, 60c.; 1½ years, 65c.; 2 years 70
2677B   **All-wool Shirts;** sizes, 3 months, 65c.; 6 months, 70c.; 9 months, 75c.; 1 year, 80c.; 1½ years, 85c.; 2 years .   .93
2677C   **Cotton Shirts,** high neck, long sleeves, or low neck and short sleeves; 3 months to 3 years . .   .25
2678   **Cream Cashmere Sacque;** infant's size to 1 year, with cream, blue or pink hand-embroidery; lined with silk 2.75
2678A   **Same as above,** unlined; cream, blue or pink silk stitching 1.35
2679   **Hand-embroidered Bib,** of nainsook 1.00
2680   **Hand-embroidered Bib,** of nainsook 2.00
2681   **Cream Cashmere Sacque;** infant's size to 1 year; hand-embroidered in cream, blue or pink . . .   1.95
2682   **Cream Knit Sacque,** all wool, with cream, blue or pink crochet edge; infant's size to 1 year . . .   1.25
2682A   **Hand-knit Sacque,** all cream, or cream with blue or pink borders; infant's size to 6 months, $2.00; 6 months to 1 year, $2.50; 1 year to 2 years, $3.00; 2 years to 3 years 3.50
2683   **Flannel Skirt,** hand-embroidered 3.25
2683A   **Similar style Skirt,** with hand-embroidered scallop   1.95
2683B   **Same as No. 2683A,** of finer flannel, $3.25 and . .   4.50
2683C   **Flannel Skirt,** with hand feather-stitched hem, 85c.   1.25
2684   **Cream Cashmere Wrapper,** collarless, hand-embroidered; colors, white, blue or pink 3.50
2685   **Cream Cashmere Sacque,** cream, blue or pink hand-embroidered scallop; infant's size to 1 year, $1.40; 2 years 1.90
2685A   **Cream Cashmere Sacque,** with cream, blue or pink silk stitching; infant's size to 1 year 1.35

INFANTS' OUTFITS

Infants' Complete Outfits can be furnished at various prices, depending upon the quality and quantity of pieces desired. Additional information in detail will be furnished upon request. We quote below three as examples:

INFANT'S OUTFIT No. 1

2686   Three Bands, at 15c. . . . . $ .45
       Three Shirts, cotton and wool, first size, at 45c. . .   1.35
       Twenty-four Cotton Bird's-eye Diapers; 2 sets, 12 pieces to set; 18 x 36 inches 1.20
       Two Pairs Bootees, at 20c. 40
       Two Barrow Coats, at 50c. 1.00
       Two Flannel Skirts, at 85c. 1.70
       Two Nainsook Skirts, at 50c. 1.00
       Three Night Slips, at 35c. 1.05
       Three Dresses, as follows: 55c., 75c., 90c. 2.20
       Two Flannelette Wrappers, at 50c. 1.00
           Forty-six Pieces $11.35

INFANT'S OUTFIT No. 2

2687   Three Bands, at 15c. . . . . $ .45
       Four Shirts, cotton and wool; 2 at 45c. first size; 2 at 50c., second size 1.90
       Thirty-six Cotton Bird's-eye Diapers; 2 sets, 12 pieces to set, 18 x 36 inches; 12 pieces, 22 x 44 inches   2.20
       Three Pairs Bootees, at 20c. 60
       Three Barrow Coats, at 50c. 1.50
       Two Flannel Skirts, at 85c. 1.70
       Three Nainsook Skirts; 2 at 50c., 1 at 70c. 1.70
       Three Night Slips, at 35c. 1.05
       Four Dresses, as follows: 55c., 70c., 90c., $1.25 . .   3.40
       Two Flannelette Wrappers, at 50c. 1.00
       One Stockinette Bath Apron 90
       Two Pique Bibs, at 25c. 50
           Sixty-six Pieces $16.90

INFANT'S OUTFIT No. 3

2688   Four Bands, at 15c. . . . . $ .60
       Four Shirts, cotton and wool; 2 at 45c., first size; 2 at 50c., second size   1.90
       Thirty-six Cotton Bird's-eye Diapers; 2 sets, 12 pieces to set, 18 x 36 inches; 12 pieces, 22 x 44 inches   2.20
       Four Pairs Bootees, at 20c. 80
       Three Barrow Coats, at 50c. 1.50
       One Shawl 90
       Three Flannel Skirts, at $1.25 . . . .   3.75
       Four Nainsook Skirts; 2 at 50c., 2 at 70c. 2.40
       Six Night Slips; 3 at 35c., 3 at 45c. 2.40
       Six Dresses, as follows: 55c., 70c., 85c., 90c., $1.25 and $1.35   5.60
       One Flannel Wrapper 1.85
       One Stockinette Bath Apron 90
       Three Pique Bibs, at 25c. 75
           Seventy-six Pieces $25.55

CHILDREN'S DRESSES AND BODY SKIRTS

2691   Lawn Dress, with embroidery and lace, beading and ribbon at waist ; sizes, 2 to 4 years . . $1.90
2692   Nainsook Dress, with embroidery insertion and ribbon ; sizes, 6 months to 3 years   . . .   1.10
2693   Nainsook Dress, hand-made and hand-embroidered ; sizes, 2 to 4 years 4.25
2694   Hand-made Nainsook Dress, with hand-embroidered yoke, real Valenciennes lace at neck
     and sleeves ; sizes, 6 months to 2½ years 2.85
2695   Hand-made Nainsook Dress, with hand-embroidered yoke and skirt, real Valenciennes lace
     at neck and sleeves ; sizes, 6 months to 2½ years 4.85
2696   Hand-made Nainsook Dress, with hand-embroidered collar ; sizes, 6 months to 2½ years   .   2.00
2697   Lawn Dress, tucks, feather-stitching and ribbon ; sizes, 2 to 4 years 1.25
2698   Hand-made Nainsook Body Skirt, Valenciennes lace edge ; sizes, 6 months to 4 years   . .   1.50
2699   Hand-made Nainsook Dress, with hand-embroidered yoke, hand-embroidered scallop around
     neck, sleeves and skirt ; sizes, 6 months to 2½ years 3.00
2700   Hand-made Nainsook Body Skirt, hand-embroidered scallop ; sizes, 6 months to 4 years   .   .90
2701   Hand-made Nainsook Dress, with embroidery, beading with ribbon at waist ; size, 2 to 4 years 1.50
2702   Poplin Dress, white, blue or pink, with white collar, cuffs and belt ; sizes, 2 to 4 years   .   1.00
2703   Girl's Chambray Bloomer Suit, trimmed with white poplin, in blue or pink ; sizes, 2 to 4 years   1.50
2704   Nainsook Dress, tucks, embroidery and Valenciennes lace ; sizes, 6 months to 2½ years   .   1.50
2705   White Piqué Dress, crochet buttons ; sizes, 2 to 4 years 1.90
2706   Lawn Dress, trimmed with insertions of embroidery and lace ; sizes, 2 to 4 years 3.25
2707   Lawn Dress, with embroidery, beading with ribbon at waist ; size, 2 to 4 years 1.50
2708   Gingham Dress, in blue and white or tan and white stripes ; sizes, 2 to 4 years 1.10
2708A Chambray Dress, white piqué collar, cuffs and belt ; sizes as above ; pink or blue 90

Body Skirts and Separate Bloomers — Not Illustrated

2709   Flannel Skirt, with machine-stitched hem ; sizes, 6 months to 3 years, 55c.; with feather-
     stitched hem, 75c. and $1.00; with hand-embroidered scallop $1.35
2710   Flannel Skirt, with scallop and dot ; sizes as above 1.85
2711   Nainsook Body Skirt, hem and tucks ; sizes as above 50
2712   Cambric Skirt, hem and tucks ; sizes, 6 months to 2½ years, 35c.; 3 years' size 40
2713   Lawn Skirt, long waist, hemstitched tucked ruffle ; sizes, 18 months to 4 years 65
2714   Same style, in nainsook, with ruffle of embroidery ; sizes, 18 months to 4 years ; 75c. . . .   1.00
2715   Separate Bloomers, for girls, white percale, also blue or pink chambray ; 2 to 4 years 50
2715A Same, in white poplin ; sizes, 2 to 4 years 85

CHILDREN'S SHORT COATS, HATS, DRESSES, ETC.

2721 Nainsook Skirt, lawn ruffle, trimmed with Valenciennes lace ; sizes, 2 to 4 years . . . . . . $ .85
2721A Similar style, embroidery ruffle and insertion ; sizes as above 90
2722 Gingham Dress, in blue and white or pink and white stripe ; sizes, 2 to 4 years 85
2723 Child's Nainsook Body Skirt, embroidery ruffle and tucks ; sizes, 6 months to 3 years 50
2723A Other styles, similar, 85c., $1.00 and 1.25
2724 Lawn Bishop Dress, beading and ribbon at neck and sleeves ; sizes, 6 months to 2½ years . . 1.00
2724A Same as above, embroidery at neck and sleeves 50
2725 Lawn Bishop Dress, smocked in blue or pink ; sizes, 6 months to 3 years 1.50
2726 Lawn Dress, embroidery and ribbon trimmed ; sizes, 2 to 4 years 2.00
2727 Nainsook Dress, tucks and feather-stitching ; sizes, 6 months to 2½ years 1.10
2727A Nainsook Dresses, embroidered yokes ; sizes, 6 months to 2½ years ; 50c. and 80
2728 Lawn Dress, with embroidery ; sizes, 6 months to 2½ years 1.10
2729 White Poplin Suit, trimmed with blue ; sizes, 2 to 4 years 2.25
2729A Similar style, in blue or brown chambray, white piqué collar, cuffs and belt ; sizes as above . 1.90
2729B White Cotton Duck Suit, collar and cuffs edged with blue embroidery ; sizes as above . . . 1.10
2730 White Twill Suit ; sizes, 2 to 4 years 1.50
2731 White Poplin Suit, straight pants, all white or white with blue ; sizes, 2 to 4 years 2.10
2732 White Piqué Coat, hand-embroidered scallop and design ; sizes, 2 to 4 years 4.75
2733 Lingerie Hat, embroidered ruffle, ribbon trimmed, blue or pink ; sizes, 2 to 4 years . . . 1.65
2734 White Piqué Coat, hand-embroidered collar and cuffs ; sizes, 6 months to 2½ years . . . 3.25
2734A Similar style, in cashmere, China silk lined 6.50
2735 Hat, of white piqué, or blue or pink poplin, to button on crown ; sizes, 6 months to 2 years . .50
2735A Similar style, with embroidery scallop, white only ; sizes as above 1.00
2736 Cream Cashmere Coat, China silk lined, hand-emb. scallop and design ; sizes, 6 mos. to 2½ yrs. 7.50
2736A Similar style, with hand-embroidered scallop on cape ; no design 4.50
2736B Cream Faille Silk Coat, cape hand-embroidered ; sizes, 6 months to 2½ years 14.50
2737 Cream Silk Poplin Cap ; sizes, infant's to 2 years 1.50
2738 Serge Reefer, sateen lined, cadet blue linen collar and cuffs ; white or navy ; sizes, 2 to 4 yrs. 6.25
2739 White Straw Hat, trimmed with navy or white velvet ribbon ; sizes, 2 to 4 years 2.00
2740 Wool Bedford Cord Coat, white batiste collar ; tan, Copenhagen, green ; sizes, 2 to 4 years . 8.00
2741 Straw Hat, trimmed with velvet ribbon and flower ; tan, Copenhagen, green ; sizes, 2 to 4 years 3.50
2742 Serge Coat, China silk lining, white piqué hand-emb. collar and cuffs, white or navy ; 2 to 4 yrs. 6.75
2743 Straw Hat, wreath of field flowers and ribbon, navy blue ; sizes, 2 to 4 years 2.00
2744 Box Coat, China silk lined, black velvet belt, white linen collar and cuffs, black and white
       check or tan serge with brown velvet belt ; sizes, 2 to 4 years 8.75
2745 White Leghorn Hat, velvet ribbon and wreath of daisies ; sizes, 2 to 4 years 5.25
2746 Serge Coat, China silk lined ; cadet or tan ; sizes, 2 to 4 years 5.75
2747 Straw Hat, velvet ribbon and flowers ; cadet with self color, tan with rose ; sizes, 2 to 4 years 2.95
2747A Straw Hat, trimmed with navy velvet ribbon, white or navy 2.25
2748 Point d'Esprit Hat, over blue or pink China silk (*not illustrated*) ; sizes, 2 to 4 years . . . 3.50

INFANTS' DRESSES, SKIRTS, LONG CLOAKS AND CAPS

2761	Hand-made Nainsook Dress, hand-embroidered yoke, lace edge and veining at neck and sleeves	$1.25
2762	Hand-made Dress, of fine nainsook, yoke and skirt hand-embroidered; lace edge and veining at neck and sleeves . .	2.85
2763	Nainsook Dress, embroidered yoke, lace edge at neck and sleeves	.85
2764	Nainsook Long Skirt, with embroidery insertion and ruffle	1.25
2764A	Nainsook Long Skirt, trimmed with embroidery (*not illustrated*)	.55
2764B	Fine Lawn Skirt, lace trimmed (*not illustrated*) . . .	1.45
2765	Hand-made Nainsook Dress, hand-embroidered yoke; lace edge and veining at neck and sleeves	1.65
2766	Nainsook Night Slip, lace at neck and sleeves	.35
2766A	Similar style, finer nainsook	.50
2766B	Same style, hand-made	.85
2766C	Finer quality	1.35
2767	Hand-made Nainsook Dress, cluster of tucks, with feather-stitching and hemstitching; lace frill at neck and sleeves . .	1.95
2767A	Hand-made Dresses, with tucks and feather-stitching (*not illustrated*), $1.00 and	1.50
2768	Nainsook Dress, embroidery yoke, skirt trimmed with embroidery and lace insertion and lace edge	1.50
2769	Nainsook Dress, cluster of tucks and veining . . .	.70
2770	Lawn Dress, embroidered yoke, skirt with ruffle of embroidery and lace insertions	1.95
2770A	Lawn Skirt, to match above dress, with embroidery ruffle .	1.10
2770B	Hand-made Nainsook Skirt, with hand-embroidered scallop at hem (*not illustrated*)	1.50
2771	Hand-made Muslin Cap; infant's to 2 yrs., 50c.; finer quality	1.00
2772	White Lawn Cap, embroidery and ribbon trimming; 6 months to 2 years	.90
2773	Sun Bonnet, of dotted muslin; sizes, 6 months to 3 years . .	1.35
2774	Hand-Made Muslin Cap, with turned back piece, with tucks and feather-stitching; infant's size to 2 years . . .	.50
2775	Infant's Long Cloak, of cream cashmere, China silk lining, hand-embroidery	6.00
2775A	Similar styles, more elaborate, $7.50, $9.75 and . . .	11.50
2775B	Same style, as No. 2775, with hand-embroidered scallop without the design, China silk lined	4.50
2775C	Infant's Long Cloak, of white crêpe de chine, cape hand-embroidered scallop	9.50
2775D	Similar styles, in faille silk, $14.50 and	19.50

Not Illustrated

2776	Infant's Cap, of net, over blue or pink silk lining; infant's size to 2 years	$1.50
2777	Infant's Cap, white crêpe de chine with turned back piece, hand-embroidered scallop; infant's size to 2 years	2.25
2778	White Pique Sun Hat, crown to button on, brim finished with a machine scallop; sizes, 1 to 2 years	1.00
2779	White Lawn Corded Sun Bonnet, lace trimmed; sizes, same as above . . .	1.00
2780	Sun Bonnet, of lawn, in white, blue or pink; sizes, 1 to 3 years	.50
2781	China Silk Cap Linings, white, blue or pink; sizes, infant's to 2 years	.35
2782	Fine Lawn Dress, trimmed with lace insertion and ruffle, $2.85; more elaborately trimmed	5.25
2783	Night Gown, of stockinet material; sizes, infant's to 2 years . . .	.65
2784	Infant's Size Night Gown, buttoned in back, of white flannelette; with a drawing string at bottom . . .	.75
2785	Same Material, in 1 year size, open in front	.85
2786	Hand-made Nainsook Night Gowns, buttoned in front; infant's size, 85c. and	1.25

RIBBON DEPARTMENT (*Prices subject to change*)

2801	Pin Wheel Bow, with knotted ends of 2-inch satin taffeta ribbon; without ribbon buds, 38c.; with buds	$ .68
2802	Pin Wheel Bow, of 5-inch satin taffeta ribbon, ribbon flowers in center, suitable for carriage cover or basket decoration	1.50
2803	Double Knotted Rosettes, of ½-inch satin taffeta ribbon, with strap between; for infants' caps and children's dresses	.90
2804	Rosette, of ¾-inch French satin, with knotted loops; pink, blue or white; suitable for children's wear, boudoir caps and dressing gowns	.35
2805	Pin Wheel Bow, suitable for lingerie and children's wear, made of 2-inch satin taffeta ribbon; without ribbon buds, 25c.; with buds	.55
2806	Knotted Rosettes, of ½-inch satin taffeta ribbon, short ends for lingerie and children's wear; without ribbon buds, 28c.; with buds	.50
2807	Knotted Shower Rosettes, of ½-inch satin taffeta ribbon, for lingerie and children's wear	.90
2808	Knotted Shower Rosettes, of ½-inch satin taffeta ribbon, for lingerie and children's wear	.50
2809	Standing Bow, for table decoration, of satin ribbon combined with fancy gauze ribbon	5.50
2810	Ribbon Rose, made of velvet, with artificial foliage	3.50
2811	Velvet Ribbon Poppy, in black, white or colors	2.25
2812	Shaded Red Satin Rose, with artificial foliage	.95
2813	Shaded Satin Apples, with artificial foliage	1.10
2814	Shaded Ribbon Violets and Foliage	2.00
2815	Cherries, combining velvet ribbon and artificial foliage	1.25

Bows, Flowers and Rosettes are made to order only

Imported Satin Taffeta and Faille Ribbons

2816	6⅜-inch Imported Satin Taffeta, kid finish, in all leading shades, yard	$ .68
2817	6¼-inch Imported Faille, for millinery or children's wear, yard	.65
2818	No. 1 B. Altman & Co.'s Special Satin Ribbon, in white, pink or blue, piece of 10 yards, yard	.15
2819	No. 1½ B. Altman & Co.'s Special Satin Ribbon, in white, pink or blue, piece of 10 yards, yard	.25

Fine French Satin Taffeta Ribbons, suitable for Sashes and Millinery Purposes

No. 40	3½ in. wide, black only, yard $ .35		No. 120	7½ in. wide, black only, yard $ .75
No. 60	4¾ in. wide, black only, yard .45		No. 150	8½ in. wide, black only, yard .95
No. 80	5¼ in. wide, black only, yard .50		No. 200	10 in. wide, black only, yard 1.25
No. 100	6⅜ in. wide, black only, yard .68			

Fancy Colored Ribbons, suitable for Undergarments and Infants' Wear

No. 1	¼ in. wide (piece only) $ .45		No. 3	¾ in. wide, yard, 11c.; piece $1.00
No. 1½	⅜ in. wide (piece only) .65		No. 5	1 in. wide, yard, 15c.; piece 1.40
No. 2	½ in. wide, yard, 8c.; piece .75		No. 9	1½ in. wide, yard, 23c.; piece 2.20

CORRECT MILLINERY

Augmenting the following list are many new and striking trimmed models in regular stock, for Women, Misses, and Girls; together with an equal number of Untrimmed Hats and every fancy which may be chosen to adorn them; also exclusive models for the most conservative

2901	Smart Tri-cornered Hat (as illustrated), in navy, black or white silk straw braid, with jaunty ribbon cockade; at the special price of	$4.75
2902	Stylish Flower Trimmed Turban (as illustrated), of fancy straw braid, in black, brown or beige; at the special price of	5.50
2903	Black, White, or Colored Fancy Feathers, $1.25, $1.90	2.75
2904	Black, White or Natural Paradise, $6.75, $12.75	22.50
2905	White, Black or Colored Ostrich Feathers, $3.50, $4.75	6.75
2906	Jet Ornaments, 75c., $1.25	1.90
2907	Small Shoulder Bouquets, also Hat Trimmings: in fruit and berries; each, 65c. and	1.00
2908	Wreaths, of fine flowers and fruit, in all leading shades and latest suggestions; each, $1.90 and	3.00
2909	Small Shoulder Roses, with foliage, in red, pink, cerise, purple or old rose; each, 50c. and	.90
2910	Large, Single La France Corsage Rose, of muslin, with bud and foliage (pink only); each, $1.00 and	1.50
2911	Untrimmed Straw Hats, $2.50, $3.75 and	5.50
2912	Girls' and Misses' Trimmed School Hats, $3.50 and	4.75
2913	Girls' and Misses' Trimmed Dress Hats, $8.50, $10.00 and	12.50
2914	Women's Trimmed Walking Hats, $5.00 and	7.50

WOMEN'S KNITTED UNDERWEAR

Every style of Knitted Undergarments for women's wear is maintained in stock and supplied in the most desirable fabrics, both of foreign and American manufacture, including all silk, silk mixed, merino and cotton. Exclusive hand-embroidered designs in French Gauze Silk Vests, also Dr. Deimel's Linen Mesh Underwear and Skirts of Flannelette, Albatross and Flannel

Especial attention is directed to the B. ALTMAN & CO. make of Merino Underwear, "BETALPH", manufactured of selected wool of fine fibre, and possessing a superior texture and finish.

Betalph

TRADE   MARK
B. A. & CO.

VESTS, Swiss Ribbed, also Italian Silk Vests and Bloomers

		Bust: 34	36	38	40	42	44	46
		Size: 28	30	32	34	36	38	40
3001	Ribbed Cotton, no straps	$ .30	$ .30	$ .30	$ .30	$ .30	$ .30	$ .30
3002	Ribbed Cotton low neck, no sleeves	.35	.35	.35	.35	.35	.35	.35
3003	Ribbed Lisle, white, low neck, no sleeves	.35	.35	.35	.35	.35	.35	.35
3004	Ribbed Lisle, no straps	.50	.50	.50	.50	.50		
3005	Ribbed Lisle, fine quality, white, low neck, no sleeves	.55	.55	.55	.55	.55	.55	.50
3006	Ribbed Lisle, fine quality, white, low neck, short sleeves	.55	.55	.55	.55	.55	.55	.55
3007	Ribbed Lisle, gauze weight, white, low neck, no sleeves	.65	.65	.65	.65	.65	.65	.65
3008	Ribbed Lisle, finest quality, white, low neck, no sleeves	1.00	1.00	1.00	1.00	1.00	1.00	1.00
3009	Ribbed Lisle, white, high neck and short sleeves	.75	.75	.75	.75	.75	.75	.75
3010	Ribbed Lisle, white, high neck and long sleeves	.85	.85	.85	.85	.85	.85	.85
3011	Ribbed Merino Wool, gauze weight, white, low neck, no sleeves	.95	.95	.95	.95	.95	.95	.95
3012	Ribbed Silk and Lisle, cream, low neck, no sleeves	.75	.75	.75	.75	.75	.85	.85
3013	Ribbed Spun Silk, fine quality, cream, low neck, no sleeves	.95	.95	.95	.95	.95	1.10	1.10
3014	Ribbed Spun Silk, gauze weight, white or pink, low neck, no sleeves	1.10	1.10	1.10	1.10	1.10	1.25	1.25
3015	Ribbed Spun Silk, finer quality, cream, low neck, no sleeves	1.35	1.35	1.35	1.35	1.35	1.50	1.50
3016	Ribbed Spun Silk, extra fine quality, cream, low neck, no sleeves	1.65	1.65	1.65	1.65	1.65	1.65	1.65
3017	**Jersey Silk Vests, tailored band top, white or pink, as illustrated ; special**	1.45	1.45	1.45	1.45	1.45	1.45	1.45
3018	Italian Silk Vests, plain, with band top, low neck, no sleeves, white or pink	2.75	2.75	2.75	2.75	2.75	2.75	
3019	Milanese Silk Vests, embroidered front, low neck, no sleeves, white or pink	2.75	2.75	2.75	2.75	2.75		
3020	Italian Silk Vests, embroidered front, Valenciennes lace edge, low neck, no sleeves, white or pink, as illustrated	3.90	3.90	3.90	3.90	3.90		
3021	Jersey Silk Bloomers, white pink, or black	1.75	1.75	1.75	1.75	1.75		
3022	Italian Silk Drawers, open or closed, white, pink or black	2.75	2.75	2.75	2.75	2.75		
3023	Italian Silk Bloomers, white, pink or black	3.75	3.75	3.75	3.75	3.75		
3024	**Fancy Jersey Silk Bloomers, white or pink, as illustrated ; special**	3.25	3.25	3.25	3.25	3.25		

MERINO VESTS

		34	36	38	40	42	44	46
3025	India Gauze, fine quality, low neck, no sleeves	$ .50	$ .50	$ .50	$ .50	$ .50	$ .60	$ .60
3026	B. Altman & Co. Brand (Betalph), fine gauze merino, full regular made, low neck, no sleeves	1.40	1.50	1.60	1.70	1.80		
3027	B. Altman & Co. Brand (Betalph), extra fine gauze merino, full regular made, low neck, no sleeves	1.80	1.90	2.00	2.10	2.20		
3028	India Gauze, fine quality, high neck, short sleeves	.50	.50	.50	.50	.50	.60	.60
3029	Fine Ribbed Cotton Shaped Vests, high neck, short sleeves	.50	.50	.50	.50	.50	.60	.60
3030	India Gauze, finer quality, full regular made, high neck, short sleeves	.85	.90	.95	1.00	1.05	1.10	1.15
3031	B. Altman & Co. Brand (Betalph), fine gauze merino, full regular made, high neck, short sleeves	1.40	1.50	1.60	1.70	1.80		
3032	India Gauze, fine quality, high neck, long sleeves	.50	.50	.50	.50	.50		
3033	Fine Ribbed Cotton Shaped Vests, high neck, long sleeves	.50	.50	.50	.50	.50	.60	.60
3034	India Gauze, finer quality, full regular made, high neck, long sleeves	.90	.95	1.00	1.05	1.10	1.15	1.20
3035	B. Altman & Co. Brand (Betalph), fine gauze merino, full regular made, high neck, long sleeves	1.50	1.60	1.70	1.80	1.90		

KNITTED UNDERWEAR FOR WOMEN—(Continued)

DRAWERS, EQUESTRIENNE TIGHTS, CORSET COVERS AND BANDS

		Bust:	34	36	38	40	42	44	46
		Size:	28	30	32	34	36	38	40
3036	India Gauze Tights, knee or ankle length		$ .50	$ .50	$ .50	$ .50	$ .50	$ .50	.50
3037	Ribbed Cotton Tights, wide leg, lace ruffle	$ .50	.50	.50	.50	.50	.50	.50	
3038	Ribbed Cotton Drawers, tight shape top, knee or ankle length	.50	.50	.50	.50	.50	.50	.60	.60
3039	Swiss Ribbed Cotton Tights, black, knee length, closed	.85	.85	.85	.85	.85	.85	.85	
3040	Swiss Ribbed Lisle Tights, fine quality, white, knee length, open	1.25	1.25	1.25	1.25	1.25	1.25	1.25	
3041	Swiss Ribbed Merino Wool Tights, gauze weight, white, knee or ankle length	1.85	1.85	1.85	1.85	1.85	1.85	1.85	
3042	Cotton Bloomers, white or black	.75	.75	.75	.75	.75	.75	.75	
3043	**Jersey Silk Corset Covers, white or pink, as illustrated; special at** . .	1.65	1.65	1.65	1.65	1.65	1.65		
3044	Ribbed Wool Bands, white or natural gray	.55	.55	.55	.55	.55	.55	.55	

WOMEN'S UNION SUITS (Vests and Drawers Combined)

3045	Ribbed Cotton, low neck, no sleeves, knee tight, or lace trimmed	$ .50	$ .50	$ .50	$ .50	$ .50	$ .50	$ .50
3046	Ribbed Cotton, better quality, low neck, no sleeves, knee tight, or lace trimmed	.75	.75	.75	.75	.75	.75	.75
3047	Ribbed Cotton, fine quality, low neck, no sleeves, knee tight, or lace trimmed .	1.00	1.00	1.00	1.00	1.00	1.25	1.25
3048	Ribbed Cotton, wide leg, lace ruffle, fine quality, low neck, no sleeves . . .	1.25	1.25	1.25	1.25	1.25	1.25	1.25
3049	Swiss Ribbed Cotton, low neck, no sleeves, knee length	1.25	1.25	1.25	1.25	1.25	1.25	1.25
3050	Ribbed Cotton, light weight, very fine quality, low neck, no sleeves, knee length	2.90	2.90	2.90	2.90	2.90	3.25	3.25
3051	Swiss Ribbed Lisle, low neck, no sleeves, knee length	1.75	1.75	1.75	1.75	1.75	1.90	1.90
3052	Swiss Ribbed, Merino Wool, gauze weight, low neck, no sleeves, knee length	2.50	2.50	2.50	2.50	2.50		
3053	**Jersey Silk, tailor band top, white or pink; special at**	2.95	2.95	2.95	2.95	2.95	2.95	2.95
3054	Italian Silk, hemstitched band, low neck, no sleeves	4.90	4.90	4.90	4.90	4.90		
3055	Italian Silk, plain, Valenciennes lace edge, low neck, no sleeves . . .	6.50	6.50	6.50	6.50	6.50		
3056	Cotton Bathing Combin. Suit, black, gray or white, knee length, as illustrated	1.00	1.00	1.00	1.00	1.00	1.00	1.00
3057	Worsted Bathing Combination Suit, black, knee length	2.25	2.25	2.25	2.25	2.25		
3058	Cotton Bathing Combination Suit, with feet, black	1.75	1.75	1.75	1.75			
3059	Worsted Bathing Combination Suit, with feet, black	3.75	3.75	3.75	3.75			

WOMEN'S MISSES' AND CHILDREN'S SWEATERS

3101 Women's and Misses' Plain Stitch Wool Sweaters, as illustrated, with large collar; white, old blue, maroon or navy; sizes, 34 to 42 . . . . . . $6.75

3102 Fancy Stitch Wool Sweaters, as illustrated; white, rose or old blue; sizes, 34 to 42 . . 5.50

3103 Fine Ribbed Silk Sweaters, as illustrated; plain white, Hague blue, Hunter green, American beauty, rose, purple, also two-toned black and white; sizes, 36 to 42 with sash, $30.00; without sash 25.00

3104 Fine Ribbed Silk Cap, to match No. 3103 . . . . 4.75

3105 Fancy Stitch Wool Sweaters, V-neck or with collar; white, gray or black; sizes, 34 to 44 4.75

3106 Plain Stitch Sweaters, heavier weight, V-neck; white, red, gray or tan; sizes, 34 to 42 . 5.75

3107 Ancona Wool Sweaters, large shawl collar and belt across back; white, rose or old blue; sizes, 36 to 42 . . . . . . 11.50

3108 Children's Plain Stitch Wool Sweaters, V-neck or with collar; white, red, tan or old blue; sizes, 26 and 28, $2.50; sizes, 30 and 32, $2.75; size, 34 . . . . 3.00

3109 Children's Fancy Stitch Wool Sweaters, with collar and belt; tan, rose or old blue; sizes, 26 and 28, $3.25; sizes, 30, 32 and size, 34 . . . . 3.50

3110 Children's Ancona Wool Sweaters, large shawl collar and belt across back; heather green and brown mixture, plain rose or delft blue; sizes, 24, 26, 28 and 30, $6.50; size, 32, $6.90; size, 34 . . . . 7.50

CORRECT TRIMMINGS FOR EVERY DEMAND OF DRESS

Not one but every fancy may be indulged in the unusual variety of Trimmings and Garnitures which embody the newest and most seasonable adaptations. Upon receipt of full information as to the desired style and approximate price, samples will be forwarded from which to make personal selection of appropriate colors and designs

3201   Crystal Bead Bugle and Rhinestone Trimming; 3¼ inches wide, yard $1.75

3206   Jet Bead Garniture, on black net $4.75

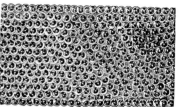

3208   Black Spangle Band; 2½ inches wide, yard $1.65
3208A Same, may be obtained in Opalescent 2.25

3202   Persian Silk and Gilt Tinsel, on black net band; 2¼ inches wide, yard $1.15

3209   Black Silk-embroidered Band, on chiffon; 2½ inches wide, yard . . . . $ .85

3203   Jet and Spangle Band, on black net; 1⅞ inches wide, yard . . $ .75

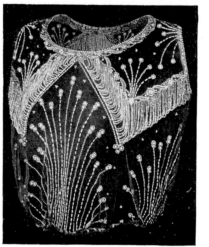

3207   Crystal Bead   Garniture, on white net, each $7.50

3210   Black Ribbozene Band; 3 inches wide, yard . . . . $ .75

3211   Amber Bead Chain Trimming, yard . . . . $ .58
3211A Same as above, in blue, pink, Bordeaux and amethyst, yard .   .58
3211B Crystal and Opalescent, yard .   .68
3211C Jet, yard 38c. and 48

3204   Silver Bugle and Rhinestone Trimming; ¾ inch wide, yard . $ .48

Dull Jet is acceptably included with the many Embroidered Crepe Trimmings for Correct Mourning Wear, both of which may be found in every acknowledged style, from 1 to 10 inches in width, ranging in price from 75c. to $10.00 a yard. Fringes and Tassels are adopted by the most conservative, and chief among the privileged white trimmings are China and Satin Beads

3205   Pink Chiffon Rosebud Trimming; ⅝-inch wide, yard . . . $ .58

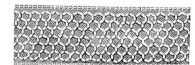

3212   White Satin Bead Band, on white net; 1⅜ inches wide, yard $ .35

Another incoming season is fulfilling its predictions in an endless variety of Spangles, Fringes, Beads, Rhinestones and Jet. Buttons of Rhinestone, Jet, Pearl, Bone and Crocheted Patterns are a dominating feature; Fringes and Tassels are striking in their varied mediums of Silk, Jet, Gilt, Crystal or Silver; and never were Spangle and Bead Garnitures more in fashionable evidence. Every Favored Trimming of the Season lends its characteristic charm to the completion of an entire array for Spring and Summer.

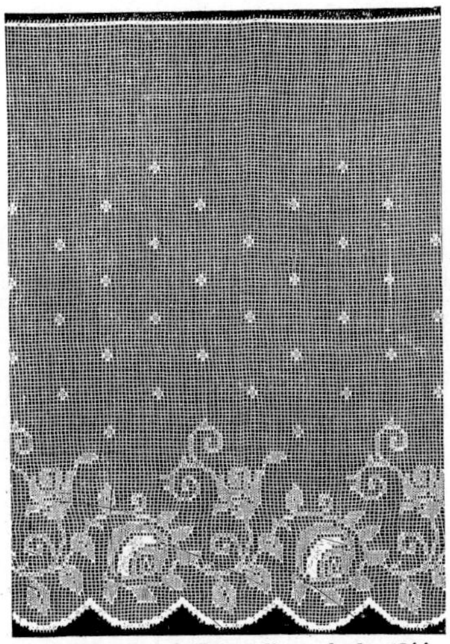

3301 **Filet Lace Edge,** linen shade, 6¾ in. wide, per yd., 40c.; 11 in. wide, per yd., 72c.; 17 in. wide, per yd., **$1.10**; 23½ in. wide, per yd., $1.45; 35 in. wide, per yd., $2.35. Inserting, 2⅜ in. wide, per yd., 14c.; 4¼ in. wide, per yd., 28c.; 7 in. wide, per yd. . . . . $ .48

VEILINGS AND ILLUSIONS

3302 **Single Hairline Veilings,** black, white or colors, per yd. . . . . $ .12
3303 **Filet and Fancy Meshes,** per yd., 25c. to . . . . $ .75
3304 **Dotted Veilings,** black, white and leading colors, per yd., 18c., 25c. to . $ .95
3305 **Hemstitched Bordered Chiffon Veils,** in various sizes, ranging in price, each, from 72c. to $3.00
Mourning Veils, in plain and fancy nets, ranging in price, each, from 68c. to . $2.25
Crape Border Veils, plain and fancy meshes, ranging in price, each, from 95c. to . $2.75
3306 **Bridal Illusions,** 3 yards wide, per yd., $1.10, $1.25 and $1.65
3307 **Bridal Illusions,** 4 yards wide, per yd., $1.45, $1.65 and $2.10

WHITE EMBROIDERIES

In our Embroidery Department is shown complete lines of Matched Sets in Cambric, Swiss, Nainsook, Batiste and Organdie Edges, Insertings and Flouncings, Matched Sets of Ribbon Beadings, also Embroidered All-overs.

3308 **Cotton Chantilly Lace Flouncing,** 18 in. wide, per yd., 48c.; 24 in. wide, per yd., 65c.; 42 in. wide, per yd. $1.10

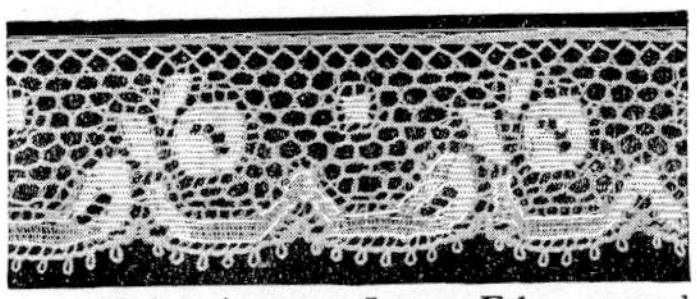

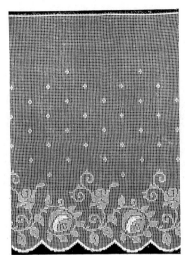

3309 **Valenciennes Lace Edge,** round mesh, ½ in. wide, per yd., 5c.; ¾ in., per yd., 6c.; 1¼ in., per yd., 9c; 2 in., per yd., 11c. Inserting, 1 in. wide per yd. . . . . $ .06

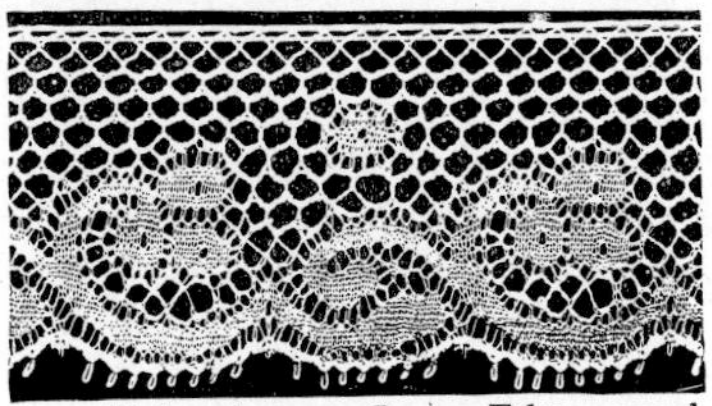

3310 **Valenciennes Lace Edge,** round mesh, ⅝ in. wide, per yd., 4c.; ⅞ in., per yd., 5c.; 1⅛ in., per yd., 6c.; 2 in., per yd., 8c. Inserting, 1 in. wide, per yd. . . . . $ .05

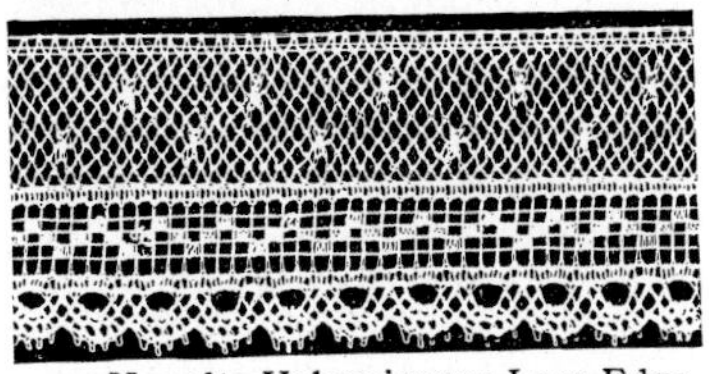

3311 **Novelty Valenciennes Lace Edge,** ⅝ in. wide, per yd., 4c.; ⅞ in., per yd., 5c.; 1 in., per yd., 6c. Inserting, ⅝ in. wide, per yd. $ .04

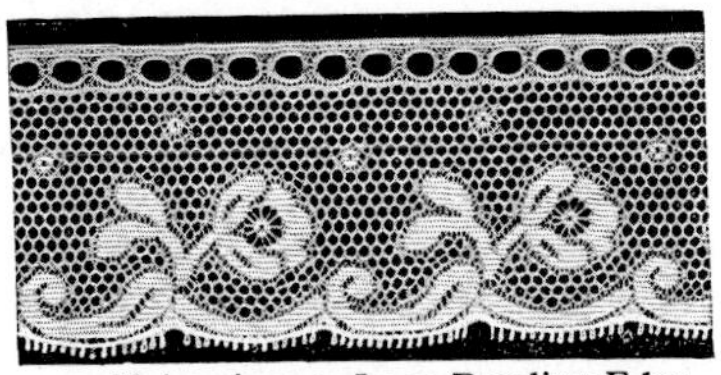

3312 **Valenciennes Lace Beading Edge,** 1 in. wide, per yd., 5c.; 1½ in., per yd., 6c.; 2⅜ in., per yd., 9c. Beading inserting, double row, 1⅛ in. wide, per yd., 5c.; 1½ in., per yd. . . . . $ .06

3313 **Platte Valenciennes Lace Edge,** round mesh, 1½ in. wide, per yd., 6c.: 3⅜ in., per yd., 12c.; 5¼ in., per yd., 18c. Inserting, 2¼ in. wide, per yd. . . . . $ .07

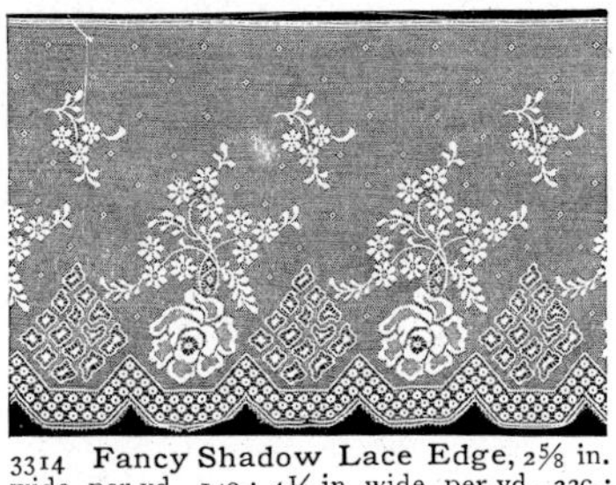

3314 **Fancy Shadow Lace Edge,** 2⅝ in. wide, per yd., 14c; 4¼ in. wide, per yd., 22c.; 7½ in. wide, per yd., 35c. Inserting, 3½ in. wide, per yd. . . . . $ .18

All illustrations represent Machine-made Goods

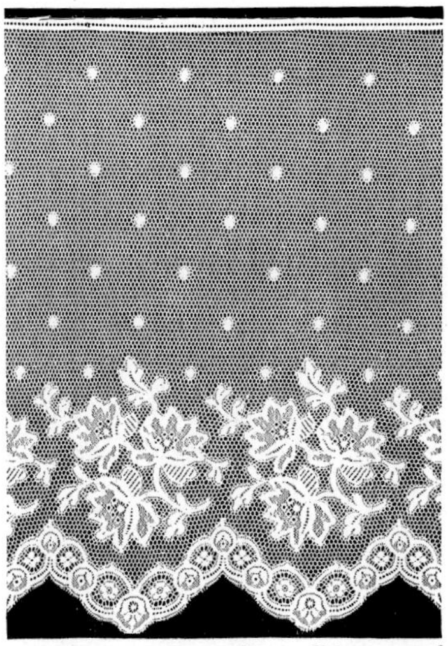

3315 **Valenciennes Lace Edge,** round mesh, in ivory and light écru, 5½ in. wide, per yd., 22c.; 11 in., per yd., 40c. Flounce, 17¼ in. wide, per yd., 62c; 22 in., per yd., 85c.; 36 in., per yd. $1.25

SILK CHIFFONS AND VOILES

42 to 45 inches wide

3316 **Chiffon,** smooth finish, black, white and complete color assortment, per yd., 75c. and 95c.; crêpe finish, per yd. $1.35
3317 **Chiffon Cloth,** black, white and leading shades, per yd., $1.50 and . . . $1.25
3318 **Voile,** sheer texture and superior durability, per yd. $1.45

SILK AND COTTON NETS

3319 **Silk Brussels Net,** in black, white and full color assortment; 48 in. wide, per yd., $1.25; 54 in. wide, per yd. $1.38
3320 **Black Silk Brussels Net,** 56 in. wide per yd., $1.10; 72 in. wide, per yd. . . $1.85
3321 **Black Silk Tosca Net,** 44 in. wide, per yd., 95c., $1.35 and $1.85
3322 **Plain Cotton Nets,** in white, cream, écru or flesh color; 54 in. wide, per yd., 48c., 65c., 78c. and $1.10; 72 in. wide, per yd, 65c., $1.10 and $1.65

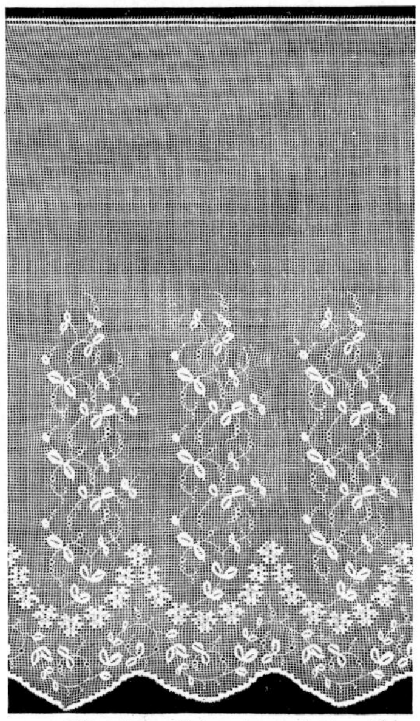

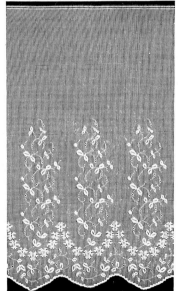

3323 **Filet Lace Edge,** ivory shade, 5¼ in. wide, per yd., 35c.; 11¼ in. wide, per yd, 68c. Flounce, 23 in. wide, per yd., $1.50; 34 in wide, per yd. $1.95

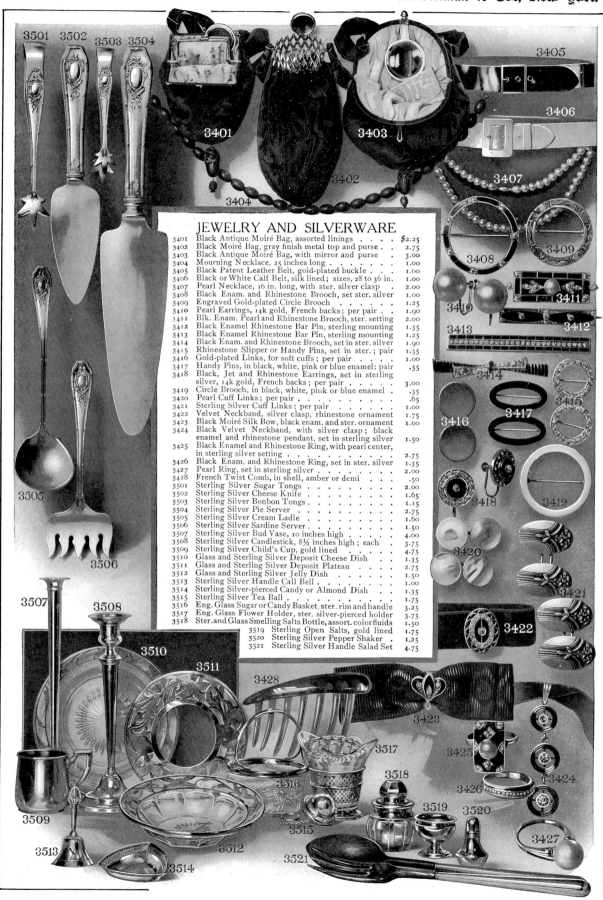

JEWELRY AND SILVERWARE

3401	Black Antique Moiré Bag, assorted linings	$2.25
3402	Black Moiré Bag, gray finish metal top and purse . .	2.75
3403	Black Antique Moiré Bag, with mirror and purse . .	3.00
3404	Mourning Necklace, 25 inches long	1.00
3405	Black Patent Leather Belt, gold-plated buckle . . .	1.00
3406	Black or White Calf Belt, silk lined; sizes, 28 to 36 in.	1.00
3407	Pearl Necklace, 16 in. long, with ster. silver clasp .	1.00
3408	Black Enam. and Rhinestone Brooch, set ster. silver	1.00
3409	Engraved Gold-plated Circle Brooch	1.25
3410	Pearl Earrings, 14k gold, French backs; per pair . .	1.90
3411	Blk. Enam. Pearl and Rhinestone Brooch, ster. setting	2.00
3412	Black Enamel Rhinestone Bar Pin, sterling mounting	1.35
3413	Black Enamel Rhinestone Bar Pin, sterling mounting	1.25
3414	Black Enam. and Rhinestone Brooch, set in ster. silver	1.90
3415	Rhinestone Slipper or Handy Pins, set in ster.; pair	1.35
3416	Gold-plated Links, for soft cuffs; per pair	1.00
3417	Handy Pins, in black, white, pink or blue enamel; pair	.55
3418	Black, Jet and Rhinestone Earrings, set in sterling silver, 14k gold, French backs; per pair	3.00
3419	Circle Brooch, in black, white, pink or blue enamel .	.35
3420	Pearl Cuff Links; per pair	.65
3421	Sterling Silver Cuff Links; per pair	1.00
3422	Velvet Neckband, silver clasp, rhinestone ornament	1.75
3423	Black Moiré Silk Bow, black enam. and ster. ornament	1.00
3424	Black Velvet Neckband, with silver clasp; black enamel and rhinestone pendant, set in sterling silver	1.50
3425	Black Enamel and Rhinestone Ring, with pearl center, in sterling silver setting	2.75
3426	Black Enam. and Rhinestone Ring, set in ster. silver	1.35
3427	Pearl Ring, set in sterling silver	2.00
3428	French Twist Comb, in shell, amber or demi . . .	.50
3501	Sterling Silver Sugar Tongs	2.00
3502	Sterling Silver Cheese Knife	1.65
3503	Sterling Silver Bonbon Tongs	1.15
3504	Sterling Silver Pie Server	2.75
3505	Sterling Silver Cream Ladle	1.60
3506	Sterling Silver Sardine Server	1.50
3507	Sterling Silver Bud Vase, 10 inches high	4.00
3508	Sterling Silver Candlestick, 8½ inches high; each .	3.75
3509	Sterling Silver Child's Cup, gold lined	4.75
3510	Glass and Sterling Silver Deposit Cheese Dish . .	1.35
3511	Glass and Sterling Silver Deposit Plateau	2.75
3512	Glass and Sterling Silver Jelly Dish	1.50
3513	Sterling Silver Handle Call Bell	1.00
3514	Sterling Silver-pierced Candy or Almond Dish . .	1.35
3515	Sterling Silver Tea Ball	1.75
3516	Eng. Glass Sugar or Candy Basket, ster. rim and handle	3.25
3517	Eng. Glass Flower Holder, ster. silver-pierced holder	3.75
3518	Ster. and Glass Smelling Salts Bottle, assort. color fluids	1.50
3519	Sterling Open Salts, gold lined	1.75
3520	Sterling Silver Pepper Shaker	1.25
3521	Sterling Silver Handle Salad Set	4.75

LEATHER GOODS, UMBRELLAS, ETC.

3601 **Envelope Pocket Book**, of morocco, in black, blue, green or brown $1.00

3602 **Hand Bag**, of pin morocco, moiré lined; containing purse and mirror; colors, black, blue, green or brown with gilt or silver trimmings; also gun-metal finish on black $2.00

3603 **Hand Bag**, of morocco, moiré lined; fitted with purse and mirror; colors, black, blue, green or brown with gilt or silver trimmings; black long grain patent leather, also gun-metal on black $2.50

3604 **Envelope Bag**, of morocco, with three compartments, moiré lined; fitted with purse and mirror; colors, black, blue, green or brown with gilt or silver trimmings; also gun-metal on black . $3.00

3605 **Hand Bag**, of crêpe grain leather, in black only, with colored moiré lining; fitted with purse and mirror, trimmed with gilt, silver or gun-metal $1.50

3606 **Key Case**, pocket, black or brown leather .75

3607 **Misses' Smart Bag**, of black long grain patent leather or ecrase grain; colors, rose, blue, green, tan or purple with gilt or silver trimmings . $1.25

3608 **Jewel or Money Pocket**, of gray suède . .45

3609 **Safety Pocket**, of gray suède; ample pockets for jewels and money $1 50

3610 **Waist Hangers**; set of six, in soft leather case of black or brown $1.75

3611 **Suitcase**, of russet sole leather, linen lined; sizes, 22 inches, $5.00; 24 inches, $5.50; 26 inches $6.00

3612 **Traveling Bag**, of black crêpe grain cowhide, leather lined; sizes, 15, 16, 17 and 18 inches $6.75

3613 **Traveling Bag**, of russet or black cowhide, with strongly riveted frame and corners; leather lined; sizes, 16, 17 and 18 inches $4.85

3614 **Suitcase**, of black-enamel duck, cretonne lined, adjustable tray and pocket in cover, durable leather corners; 18 inches long, 14 inches wide and 8 inches deep; special $4.90

3615 **Collar Bag**, of soft black or brown leather $1.00

3616 **Coin Purse**, of morocco, in black or colors $ 50

3617 **Bill Fold**, of black pin seal, calf lined . 1.00

3618 **Bill Case**, black seal, with memorandum 2.00

3619 **Writing Case**, of morocco, in black, blue, green, purple; roomy compartments; lock and key $3.75

3620 **Dressing Case for Men**, black grain leather with leather lining; fitted with real ebony-back military brush; metal tubes for shaving brush and soap; bottle containing tooth and nail brush, comb and large leather covered mirror $4.75

3621 **Dressing Case for Women**, black morocco; with celluloid fittings and colored moiré lining . $5.00

3622 **Aluminum Drinking Cup**; set of three, leather case $1.00

3623 **Drinking Glass**, in leather case 95

3624 **Medicine Case**, of black grain leather, very compact, with nickel screw-top bottles . . $1.25

3701 **Floral Silk Parasol**, with shirred edge; pink or blue flowers 5.50

3702 **Parasolette**, hemstitched border, folding handle; in black and colors $3.50

3703 and 3704 **Taffeta Sun Umbrella**, rainproof, handle of natural wood, crook shape or small silver cap; navy, purple, green or black; 24-in. . $3.50

3705 **Bell Shape Taffeta Parasol**, in black and all staple colors with novelty handle of colored bakelite in mushroom shape top $4.75

3706 **Parasol**, of taffeta silk, with folding mission handle; measures when folded 26 inches; in black and all staple colors $3.85

3707 **Parasol, taffeta silk, shirred edge, carved stick; all the season's colors; special $2.85**

3708 **Black and White 1-inch Stripe Silk Parasol**, with black stick $3.50

3709 **Rainproof Taffeta Parasol**, partridge wood stick with Prince of Wales handle; purple, green, navy, black; 22-in. (*not illustrated*) $6.50

STATIONERY DEPARTMENT

3801 Guest Book, Morocco, with spaces allotted for name, residence, arrival, departure and remarks $3.00
3802 Hasty Line Pad, sheet and envelope combined, in a Morocco case 85
3803 "Places Visited", Morocco book, in various colors, for recording items of interest while traveling 1.25
3804 Family Laundry Lists, in black leather case, 85c.; additional refills for same, each 35
3805 Autograph Albums, in Morocco leather 75
3806 Scholar's Companion, containing an assortment of pencils, pens, erasers, ruler, pencil sharpener, etc. 95
3807 "Books I Have Read"—a Morocco book register, with spaces for author, title, date and remarks 75
3808 Telephone List, of leather, disc shaped to fit on mouthpiece; black or colors 2.00
3809 Writing Tablets, containing 100 sheets, with 100 envelopes, tissue lined, in the various colors to match 1.00
3810 Boxes, containing 4 quires of white paper, and 1 quire of correspondence cards, with envelopes for both 85
3811 Children's Party Invitations, in boxes containing 24 cards and 24 envelopes 45
3812 Birth Announcements, white, with pink or blue border, in boxes containing 24 sheets and 24 envelopes 45
3813 Correspondence Cards, in boxes containing 24 cards and 24 envelopes 25
3814 "Small Memo", ecrase leather, in desirable colors, with two additional refills 65
3815 Shopping List, in various colors of Morocco, with two additional refills 45
3816 B. Altman & Co.'s Fountain Pen, with gold pen point 90
3817 Pencil Sets, containing 1 silver holder and 6 pencils with erasers .75
3818 Silver Filigree Fountain Pen 2.50

STATIONERY AND ENGRAVING

Complete facilities are afforded for executing Wedding Stationery for invitations, announcements, anniversaries and receptions; also correct Stationery for private occasions or social entertainments, Visiting and Correspondence Cards. Sample book sent upon request.

Monograms and Address Dies—Illustrated

Die, Style No. 206, for first 15 letters or less, $1.25; each additional letter or numeral . . . . $ .08
Die, Style No. 209, first 15 letters or less, $2.00; each additional letter or numeral 13
Die, Style No. 8, first 15 letters or less, $1.25; each additional letter or numeral 08
Die, Style No. 17, first 15 letters or less, $1.75; each additional letter or numeral 10
Die, Style No. 113 . . . . 2.00

Die, Style No. 199	$2.50	Die, Style No. 109	$2.50
Die, Style No. 133	3.50	Die, Style No. 123	2.00
Die, Style No. A23	3.50	Die, Style No. 111	2.00

Not Illustrated

3819 Boxes, containing 5 quires paper and 100 envelopes; white, smooth finish, 60c.; blue, gray or white lawn finish . . . $ .75
3820 Cabinet of Danish Cloth, 5 quires paper and 100 envelopes, two sizes; in blue, gray or white 75
3821 Cabinet of Empire Linen, 5 quires paper and 100 envelopes, note size; white only 90

Mourning Papers, Cards, Etc.—Not Illustrated

3822 Playing Cards, ranging in price, per pack, from 18c. to . . . $ .75
3823 Box of Mourning Paper, 1 quire and envelopes, borders 1-2-3 .35
3824 Large square size, borders 1-2-3 40
3825 Large square size, border 5 45
3826 Box of Correspondence Cards, 1 quire, borders 1-2-3 45
3827 Same as above, border 5 50
3828 Cabinet of Mourning Paper, 5 quires and 100 envelopes; two sizes; borders 0-1-2-3 . . . . 1.50
Full line of Score Pads, Bridge, Tally and Place Cards maintained in stock.

B. Altman & Co. Water-marked Papers with Envelopes

3829 Small note size, per quire, 35c.; 5 quires $1.60
3830 Medium note size, per quire, 35c.; 5 quires 1.60
3831 Square letter size, per quire, 50c.; 5 quires 2.25

3832 *Script* Plate, including 50 cards, name only . . . 1.00

3833 **Black Old English** Plate, bearing 15 letters or less in name, and 50 cards 2.00

3834 Each additional letter in name, address or reception day . . .10

3835 **Shaded Old English** Plate, bearing 15 letters or less in name, and 50 cards 3.00

3836 Each additional letter in name, address or reception day . . .15

3837 **Shaded Roman** Plate, bearing 15 letters or less in name, and 50 cards . . . 3.00

3838 Each additional letter in name, address or reception day . . .15

Stamping

3839 Paper (only), per quire, in one color; red, blue, black, gray $ .10
3840 White, per quire, 20c.; gold, silver or bronzes, burnished .20
3841 Two-color illuminations, per quire, styles 111 and 113, 50c.; 133 and A23 75

NOTE—Engraving orders should be accompanied by remittance, except where patrons have an account. For safety and convenience we retain and register plates and dies, subject to order of owner, unless otherwise directed when order is placed. Ten days to two weeks required to fill orders for engraving. Mourning orders given prompt attention

BY THE WAY
YORK HARBOUR MAINE
206
5 EAST 41ST STREET
17
44 EAST 50TH STREET
209
VILLA FRANCESCA
SETAUKET LONG ISLAND
8
M.M.B.
109
199
123
A 23
133
111
113

FANCY NEEDLEWORK DEPARTMENT

Spring and Summer make an especial appeal to the embroiderer, and not only must the Little Folk have daintily embroidered Frocks, Hats, Caps, Afghans and Pillow Covers, but the Grown-ups are obsessed with the warm-weather enthusiasm for Embroidered Blouses, Crisp Cuff and Collar Sets, Delicate Lingerie and Fascinating Boudoir Garments. All these are maintained in a wide and charming range; not forgetting the Luncheon Sets, Convenient Bags, Towels and Linen Accessories, Etc. Embroidery Ribbons, Silks and Cottons in all shades and colors, with every conceit in wool and cotton for the knitting and crochet devotee.

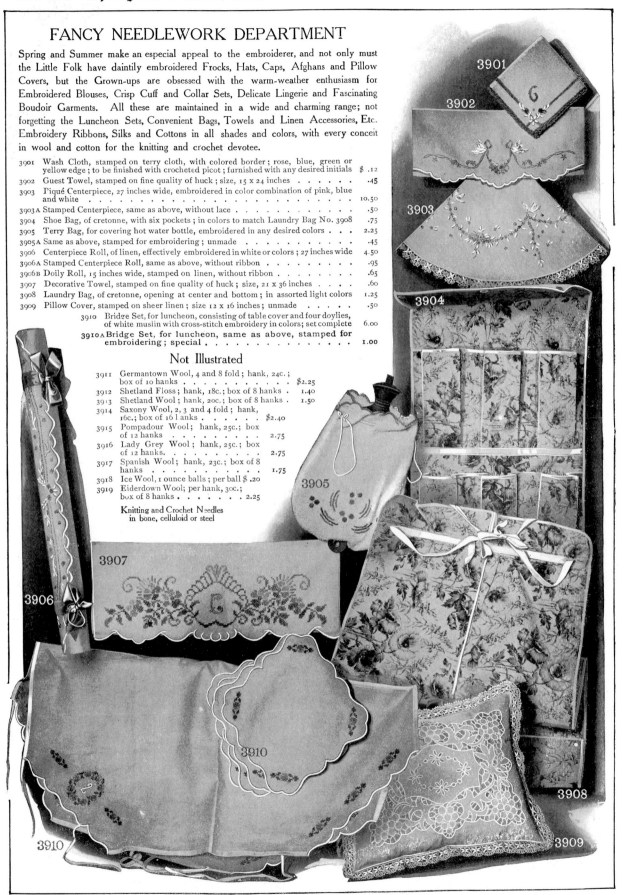

3901	Wash Cloth, stamped on terry cloth, with colored border; rose, blue, green or yellow edge; to be finished with crocheted picot; furnished with any desired initials	$ .12
3902	Guest Towel, stamped on fine quality of huck; size, 15 x 24 inches	.45
3903	Piqué Centerpiece, 27 inches wide, embroidered in color combination of pink, blue and white	10.50
3903A	Stamped Centerpiece, same as above, without lace	.50
3904	Shoe Bag, of cretonne, with six pockets; in colors to match Laundry Bag No. 3908	.75
3905	Terry Bag, for covering hot water bottle, embroidered in any desired colors . . .	2.25
3905A	Same as above, stamped for embroidering; unmade	.45
3906	Centerpiece Roll, of linen, effectively embroidered in white or colors; 27 inches wide	4.50
3906A	Stamped Centerpiece Roll, same as above, without ribbon	.95
3906B	Doily Roll, 15 inches wide, stamped on linen, without ribbon	.65
3907	Decorative Towel, stamped on fine quality of huck; size, 21 x 36 inches	.60
3908	Laundry Bag, of cretonne, opening at center and bottom; in assorted light colors	1.25
3909	Pillow Cover, stamped on sheer linen; size 12 x 16 inches; unmade	.50
3910	Bridge Set, for luncheon, consisting of table cover and four doylies, of white muslin with cross-stitch embroidery in colors; set complete	6.00
3910A	Bridge Set, for luncheon, same as above, stamped for embroidering; special	1.00

Not Illustrated

3911	Germantown Wool, 4 and 8 fold; hank, 24c.; box of 10 hanks	$2.25
3912	Shetland Floss; hank, 18c.; box of 8 hanks .	1.40
3913	Shetland Wool; hank, 20c.; box of 8 hanks .	1.50
3914	Saxony Wool, 2, 3 and 4 fold; hank, 16c.; box of 16 hanks	$2.40
3915	Pompadour Wool; hank, 25c.; box of 12 hanks	2.75
3916	Lady Grey Wool; hank, 25c.; box of 12 hanks.	2.75
3917	Spanish Wool; hank, 23c.; box of 8 hanks	1.75
3918	Ice Wool, 1 ounce balls; per ball $ .20	
3919	Eiderdown Wool; per hank, 30c.; box of 8 hanks	2.25

Knitting and Crochet Needles in bone, celluloid or steel

MARVEX GLOVES
FOR MEN, WOMEN AND CHILDREN

The **MARVEX** Gloves are made exclusively for B. Altman & Co., by Trefoussé et Cie, of Chaumont, France. Only the choicest skins are used; their excellent quality, marked durability and correct style are assured. In addition to a large assortment meeting the correct requirements for street wear, they may be found in every shade and length appropriate for evening or semi-dress demand.

Women's MARVEX Suède

4001	Marvex, 3 clasps, embroidered, black or colors	$2.00
4002	Marvex, 2 buttons, embroidered, black or white	2.00
4003	Marvex, 2 clasps, embroidered, piqué-sewn, black or white	2.25
4004	Marvex, 8 buttons, Mousquetaire, black, white or colors	2.25
4005	Marvex, 12 buttons, Mousquetaire, black, white or colors	3.00
4006	Marvex, 16 buttons, Mousquetaire, black, white or colors	3.50
4007	Marvex, 20 buttons, Mousquetaire, black, white or colors, and opera shades	4.25
4008	Marvex, 24 buttons, Mousquetaire, black, white or colors	5.00

Men's MARVEX

4009	Marvex, Glacé, piqué-sewn, 1 clasp, embroidered black or tans	$2.25
4010	Marvex, Glacé, 1 button, embroidered, white	2.25
4011	Marvex, Suède, piqué-sewn, 1 clasp or 1 button, embroidered, grays or pearls	2.25

Women's MARVEX Glacé

4012	Marvex, 3 clasps, embroidered, black, white or colors	$2.00
4013	Marvex, 2 clasps, embroidered, piqué-sewn, black, white or colors	2.25
4014	Marvex, 8 buttons, Mousquetaire, black, white or colors	2.75
4015	Marvex, 12 buttons, Mousquetaire, black, white or colors	3.50
4016	Marvex, 16 buttons, Mousquetaire, black, white or colors	4.00
4017	Marvex, 20 buttons, Mousquetaire, black or white	5.00
4018	Marvex, 24 buttons, Mousquetaire, black or white	5.50
4019	Marvex, 16 buttons, Mousquetaire, extra large arms, black or white	4.75
4020	Marvex, 20 buttons, Mousquetaire, extra large arms, black or white	5.75

Children's MARVEX

4021	Marvex, Misses' Glacé, 2 clasps, embroidered, black, white or colors	$1.75
4022	Marvex, Boys' Glacé, 1 clasp, piqué-sewn, white or tan	1.75
4023	Marvex, Boys' Suède, 1 clasp, piqué-sewn, grays	1.75

WOMEN'S GLOVES

Doeskin-finish Chamois Gloves (Washable)

4024	1 or 2 buttons, white or natural	$1.50
4025	8 buttons, Mousquetaire, white or natural	2.00
4026	12 buttons, Mousquetaire, white or natural	2.25
4027	16 buttons, Mousquetaire, white or natural	3.00

Chamois Gloves (Washable)

4028	1 button, prix-seam, white or natural	$1.00
4029	8 buttons, white or natural	1.50
4030	16 buttons, white or natural	2.25

Suède Gloves

4031	Alpa, 2 buttons, black, white or colors	$1.35
4032	Perault, 2 clasps, piqué-sewn, colors	1.75
4033	Perault, 8 buttons, Mousquetaire, black, white or colors	2.00
4034	Perault, 16 buttons, Mousquetaire, black, white or colors	3.00

Mocha, Buckskin and Golf Gloves

4035	Mocha, 1 clasp, tan or gray	$1.00
4036	Mocha, 1 clasp, prix-seam, slate, $1.50	2.00
4037	Mocha, 2 clasps, piqué-sewn, tan or slate, $1.50	2.00
4038	Mocha, 8 buttons, Mousquetaire, slate	2.25
4039	Buckskin, 1 button, white	2.00
4040	Regulation Golf, white, $1.50 and	2.00

Cape Gloves and Gauntlets

4041	Cape, prix-seam, 1 clasp, black, tan or white, $1.00, $1.50	$2.00
4042	Cape, prix-seam, 8 buttons, Mousquetaire, black, tan or white	2.25
4043	Grip Driving Gloves, 1 button, tan	2.25
4044	Glacé Gauntlets, black, tan or white	1.75
4045	Cape Gauntlets, soft cuffs, black or tan	3.00

Glacé Gloves

4046	Biarritz, 6-button length, black, white or tan	$1.00
4047	Voca, 2 clasps, overseam, black, white or colors	1.00
4048	Voca, 1 clasp, piqué, black, white or colors	1.15
4049	Alpa, 2 clasps, black, white or colors	1.45
4050	Perault, 2 clasps, black, white or colors	1.60
4051	8 buttons, Mousquetaire, black or white	1.75
4052	Perault, 8 buttons, Mousquetaire, black or white	2.25
4053	Glacé, 12 buttons, Mousquetaire, black or white	2.25
4054	Perault, 12 buttons, Mousquetaire, black or white	3.00
4055	Glacé, 16 buttons, Mousquetaire, black or white	2.75
4056	Perault, 16 buttons, Mousquetaire, black or white	3.50
4057	Glacé, 20 buttons, Mousquetaire, white	3.50
4058	Perault, 20 buttons, Mousquetaire, black or white	4.50

Silk and Mesh Gloves

4059	Silk, double finger-tips, 2 clasps, black, tan, gray or white, 50c., 75c. and	$1.00
4060	Silk, extra heavy quality, double finger-tips, 2 buttons or clasps, embroidered, black or white	1.25
4061	Silk, 8 buttons, Mousquetaire, black, tan, gray or white	1.00
4062	Silk, 12 buttons, Mousquetaire, black, tan, gray or white	1.25
4063	Silk, 16 buttons, Mousquetaire, black, white or colors, $1.00 and	1.50
4064	Mesh, 2 clasps, black or white, 75c., $1.00 and	1.25
4065	Mesh, 16 buttons, Mousquetaire, black or white, $1.50 and	2.25

Lisle, Chamois Lisle and Duplex Gloves

4066	Suède Lisle, 2 clasps, black or white, 38c., 50c. and	$ .75
4067	Lisle, 8 buttons, Mousquetaire, black or white	1.00
4068	Lisle, 16 buttons, Mousquetaire, black or white, 75c. and	1.50
4069	Chamois Lisle, 2 clasps, gray, yellow or white, 50c. and	.75
4070	Chamois Lisle, 16 buttons, Mousquetaire, white or yellow, $1.00 and	1.50
4071	Duplex Gloves, 2 clasps, white, gray or yellow	1.00
4072	Elbow-length Silk Mitts, plain or open-work, black or white	1.00

MEN'S GLOVES

Qualities and Makes in Men's Glacé, Suède, Cape, Buck, Mocha, Doeskin-finish Chamois, and Chamois (Washable); also Gauntlets

4073	Chamois, prix-seam, 1 button, natural	$1.00
4074	Doeskin-finish Chamois, 1 button, white or natural	1.50
4075	Golf, chamois, 1 button, white	1.50
4076	Cape, 1 clasp, tan	1.00
4077	Cape, 1 clasp, tan, $1.50 and	2.00
4078	Glacé, 1 button, embroidered, white	1.15
4079	Glacé 1 clasp, tans, $1.50	1.90
4080	Mocha, 1 clasp, slate	1.25
4081	Mocha, prix-seam, slate, $1.50	2.00
4082	Mocha, piqué-sewn, 1 clasp, black, tan or slate	2.00

4083	Cape, prix-seam, strap wrist, black or tan	$2.00
4084	Cape Grip, driving gloves, 1 button, tan	2.50

Men's Gauntlets

4085	Cape Gauntlets, black or tan, $2.00	$3.75
4086	Buckskin Gauntlets	2.25

Men's Fabric Gloves

4087	Silk, 1 clasp, tans and grays	$1.00
4088	Silk Mesh, 1 clasp, tans or grays	1.35
4089	Tropical, 1 clasp, mesh back, glacé palm, tan	1.75
4090	Lisle, 1 clasp, slate or tans	.75
4091	Chamois Lisle, 1 button, yellow, slate or white	.50
4092	Duplex, 1 button, yellow, slate or white	1.00

CHILDREN'S GLOVES

Qualities in Glacé, Suède, Cape, Mocha and Doeskin-finish Chamois (Washable); also Gauntlets

4093	Glacé, 1 clasp, tan or white	$1.00
4094	Misses' Voca, Glacé, 2 clasps, white or tan	1.00
4095	Cape, prix-seam, 1 clasp, tan or white, $1.00	1.50
4096	Doeskin-finish Chamois, washable, white or natural, $1.00	1.25
4097	Mocha, 1 clasp, tan or slate, $1.15	1.50
4098	Misses' Alpa Glace, 16 buttons, black, tan or white	3.00
4099	Misses' Perault Suède, 16 buttons, Mousquetaire, white	2.25
4100	Military Buckskin Gauntlets	1.50

Fabric Gloves

4101	Silk, 2 clasps, black, tan or gray	$ .50
4102	Silk, 2 buttons, white, 50c. and	.75
4103	Silk, 12 buttons, Mousquetaire, white, pink or blue	.75
4104	Lisle, 2 clasps, white, tan or gray	.38
4105	Lisle, 1 clasp, white or tan, 25c. and	.50
4106	Chamois Lisle, 1 clasp, tan, gray, yellow or white	.50

When ordering gloves for children it is requested that age as well as size be stated

Glove Stretchers, each, 65c.; Powder Boxes, 85c.; Glovina Blacking, 15c.; Soltaires and Extension Clasps, per pair, 10c.
Forms for Washing or Drying Gloves, 35c. each

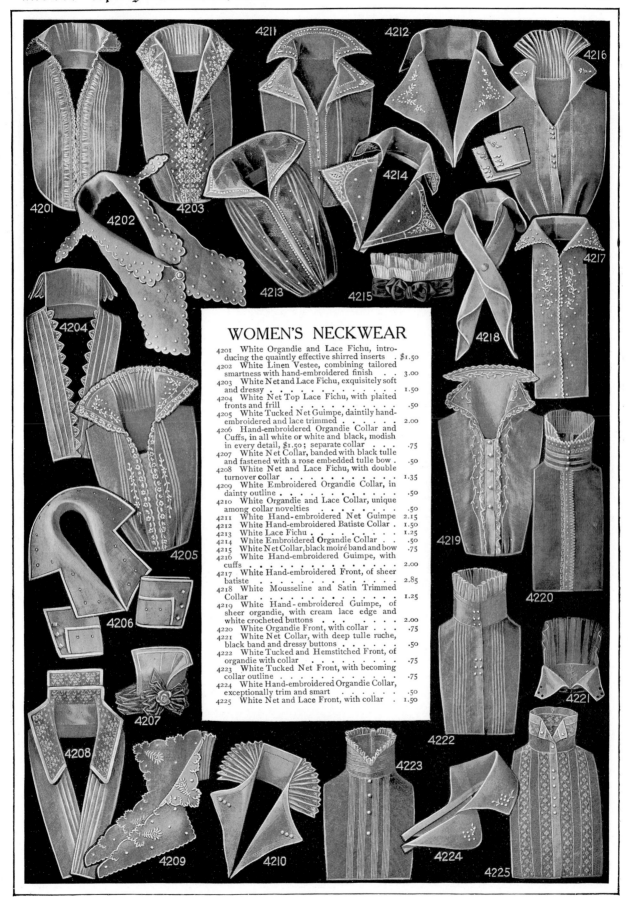

WOMEN'S NECKWEAR

4201 White Organdie and Lace Fichu, introducing the quaintly effective shirred inserts . $1.50
4202 White Linen Vestee, combining tailored smartness with hand-embroidered finish . . 3.00
4203 White Net and Lace Fichu, exquisitely soft and dressy 1.50
4204 White Net Top Lace Fichu, with plaited fronts and frill 50
4205 White Tucked Net Guimpe, daintily hand-embroidered and lace trimmed 2.00
4206 Hand-embroidered Organdie Collar and Cuffs, in all white or white and black, modish in every detail, $1.50; separate collar . . .75
4207 White Net Collar, banded with black tulle and fastened with a rose embedded tulle bow . .50
4208 White Net and Lace Fichu, with double turnover collar 1.35
4209 White Embroidered Organdie Collar, in dainty outline 50
4210 White Organdie and Lace Collar, unique among collar novelties 50
4211 White Hand-embroidered Net Guimpe . 2.15
4212 White Hand-embroidered Batiste Collar . 1.50
4213 White Lace Fichu 1.25
4214 White Embroidered Organdie Collar . . .50
4215 White Net Collar, black moiré band and bow .75
4216 White Hand-embroidered Guimpe, with cuffs 2.00
4217 White Hand-embroidered Front, of sheer batiste 2.85
4218 White Mousseline and Satin Trimmed Collar 1.25
4219 White Hand-embroidered Guimpe, of sheer organdie, with cream lace edge and white crocheted buttons 2.00
4220 White Organdie Front, with collar 75
4221 White Net Collar, with deep tulle ruche, black band and dressy buttons 50
4222 White Tucked and Hemstitched Front, of organdie with collar 75
4223 White Tucked Net Front, with becoming collar outline 75
4224 White Hand-embroidered Organdie Collar, exceptionally trim and smart 50
4225 White Net and Lace Front, with collar . 1.50

BLANKETS, COMFORTABLES AND BEDSPREADS
ALSO COTTON SHEETS, PILLOW AND BOLSTER CASES, DOMESTIC COTTON CLOTHS, CAMBRIC, ETC.

For Summer use the lighter weight Bed Coverings, such as Summer Blankets, Comfortables, Dimity and Light Weight Satin Bedspreads, are shown in an exceptional variety as enumerated below, particular attention being directed to the moderate prices

Bedding dimensions as quoted are approximate

Summer Weight Blankets

4300	36 x 50 inches, pair	$3.00 and	. . . .	$4.00
4301	42 x 56 inches, pair	3.75 and	. . . .	5.00
4302	60 x 80 inches, pair	3.50 to	. . . .	6.00
4303	72 x 84 inches, pair	3.25 to	. . . .	12.50
4304	80 x 90 inches, pair	5.50 to	. . . .	15.00
4305	90 x 90 inches, pair	10.00 and	. . . . . .	14.50

Crib Blankets, regular weight, blue or pink borders

4306	30 x 40 inches, pair	$1.50 to	. . . .	$5.00
4307	36 x 50 inches, pair	2.50 to	. . . .	6.75
4308	42 x 56 inches, pair	3.75 to	. . . .	8.00
4309	48 x 64 inches, pair	4.75 to	. . . .	9.50

For Camping and Out-door Purposes, a complete assortment of Blankets in Gray and Scarlet; also Army Blankets

4310	Gray Blankets, 60 x 80 inches, pair	$2.00 to	. . . . .	$8.75
4311	Gray Blankets, 70 x 80 inches, pair	3.00 to	. . . . .	10.00
4312	Scarlet Blankets, 60 x 80 inches, pair	5.00 to	. . . .	8.75
4313	Scarlet Blankets, 70 x 80 inches, pair	6.00 to	. . . .	10.00
4314	Army Blankets, 66 x 84 inches, each	4.00 and	. . . . .	5.00

Lamb's Wool-filled Comfortables, covered with figured silk center, finished with plain silk border and back

4315	Cut size, 36 x 48 inches, each	. . . .	$6.00
4316	Cut size, 48 x 60 inches, each	. . . .	8.00
4317	Cut size, 72 x 78 inches, each, $10.00 and	. . . . . .	13.50

Plain Colored Comfortables, with Lamb's Wool Fillings; silk, satin or dotted mull coverings, in a variety of shades

4318	Dotted Mulls, cut size, 72 x 84 inches, each	. . . .	$7.50
4319	Plain Silks, cut size, 72 x 78 inches, each, $12.50 and	. . .	15.50
4320	Plain Satins, cut size, 72 x 78 inches, each	. . . . .	18.00

Lamb's Wool-filled Comfortables, with figured mull center and plain mull border; figured silkoline back to match

4321	Cut size, 72 x 78 inches, each	. . . .	$5.50

Lamb's Wool-filled Comfortables, with both sides of figured silkoline

4322	Cut size, 72 x 78 inches, each	. . . .	$3.25

Cotton-filled Comfortables, with both sides of figured silkoline

4323	Cut size, 72 x 78 inches, each, $1.50 to	. . . . . .	$2.50

Cotton-filled Comfortables, with figured mull center and plain mull border; figured silkoline back to match

4324	Cut size, 72 x 78 inches, each, $3.00 and	. . . .	$3.75

Crib Screens or Draught Shields, covered with extra quality plain quilted sateen, in pale blue, light pink or all white

4325	Set of 4 pieces	. . . .	$6.00

Quilted Mattress Protectors

4326	18 x 34 inches, each	. . . .	$ .26
4327	27 x 40 inches, each	. . . .	.45
4328	34 x 52 inches, each	. . . .	.68
4329	36 x 76 inches, each	. . . .	1.05
4330	42 x 76 inches, each	. . . .	1.15
4331	48 x 76 inches, each	. . . .	1.25
4332	54 x 76 inches, each	. . . .	1.45
4333	60 x 76 inches, each	. . . .	1.55
4334	68 x 76 inches, each	. . . .	1.75

Crochet Bedspreads

4335	Small size, each	$1.00 to	. . . . . .	$1.60
4336	Medium size, each	1.00 to	. . . . . .	1.90
4337	Large size, each	2.00 and	. . . . .	2.50

Patent Satin Bedspreads

4338	Small size, each	$2.50 to	. . . . .	$13.00
4339	Medium size, each	3.00 to	. . . . .	10.50
4340	Large size, each	3.75 to	. . . . .	18.00

All White Corded or Crinkled Dimity Bedspreads

4341	62 x 90 inches, each	. . . .	$1.10
4342	72 x 90 inches, each	. . . .	1.20
4343	80 x 90 inches, each	. . . .	1.30

All White Corded Dimity Bedspreads, extra length

4344	72 x 99 inches, each	. . . .	$2.50
4345	90 x 99 inches, each	. . . .	3.25

All White Crinkled Dimity Bedspreads, extra length and quality

4346	72 x 99 inches, each	. . . .	$1.65
4347	90 x 99 inches, each	. . . .	2.00

Figured All White Aerial Satin Bedspreads, extra length

4348	72 x 99 inches, each	. . . .	$2.75
4349	90 x 99 inches, each	. . . .	3.50

Scalloped Edge Bedspreads, straight or cut corners

4350	All White Corded Dimity, for 3-feet or 3-feet 6-inch beds, each		$3.00
4351	All White Corded Dimity, for 4-feet 6-inch beds, each	. . .	3.75
4352	All White Aerial Satin, for 3-feet or 3-feet 6-inch beds, each	.	3.25
4353	All White Aerial Satin, for 4-feet 6-inch beds, each	. . . .	4.00
4354	Patent Satin, for 3-feet or 3-feet 6-inch beds, each, $3.25 to	.	14.00
4355	Patent Satin, for 4-feet 6-inch beds, each, $4.00 to	. . .	19.00

All White Crinkled Dimity Bedspreads, with scalloped edges, straight or cut corners. Pillow Shams and Bolster Roll of same scalloped material

4356	Shams, 36 x 36 inches, each .	. . . . . .	$ .55
4357	Bolster Roll, 36 x 72 inches, each	. . . . . .	.85
4358	Bedspreads, for 3-feet or 3-feet 6-inch beds, each	. . . .	2.15
4359	Bedspreads, for 4-feet 6-inch beds, each	. . . .	2.50

COTTON SHEETS AND PILLOW CASES
Prices subject to change

Plain Hem Cotton Pillow Cases

4400	42 inches, each	$ .18 to	. . . . . .	$ .32
4401	45 inches, each	.20 to	. . . . . .	.36
4402	50 inches, each	.24 to	. . . . . .	.40
4403	54 inches, each	.27 to	. . . . . .	.41

Hemstitched Cotton Pillow Cases

4404	42 inches, each	$ .28 to	. . . . .	$ .40
4405	45 inches, each	.30 to	. . . . .	.44
4406	50 inches, each	.34 to	. . . . .	.48
4407	54 inches, each	.38 to	. . . . .	.49

Plain Hem Cotton Bolster Cases

4408	42 inches, each	$ .38 to	. . . . .	$ .54
4409	45 inches, each	.48 to	. . . . .	.65

Hemstitched Cotton Bolster Cases

4410	42 inches, each	$ .50 to	. . . . .	$ .68
4411	45 inches, each	.60 to	. . . . .	.78

Plain Hem Cotton Sheets

4412	1½ x 2⅛ yards, each	$ .62 to	. . . . .	$ .82
4413	1½ x 2¾ yards, each		. . . . .	1.00
4414	1¾ x 2½ yards, each	.65 and	. . . .	.70
4415	2 x 2½ yards, each		. . . . .	.78
4416	2 x 2¾ yards, each	.78 and	. . . .	.85
4417	2¼ x 2¾ yards, each	.85 and	. . . .	.95
4418	2½ x 2¾ yards, each	.95 to	. . . .	1.58

Extra Length Plain Hem Sheets

4419	1¾ yards wide, each	$ .75 to	. . . . .	$1.48
4420	2 yards wide, each	.85 to	. . . . .	1.78
4421	2¼ yards wide, each	.92 to	. . . . .	1.80

4422	2½ yards wide, each	$1.00 to	. . . . .	$1.88
4423	2¾ yards wide, each	1.56 to	. . . .	2.12

Hemstitched Cotton Sheets

4424	1½ x 2⅛ yards, each	$ .68 to	. . . . .	$ .90
4425	1½ x 2¾ yards, each		. . . . .	1.20
4426	1¾ x 2⅞ yards, each	1.05 to	. . . .	1.54
4427	2 x 2⅞ yards, each	1.15 to	. . . .	1.80
4428	2¼ x 2¾ yards, each	1.20 and	. . .	1.52
4429	2¼ x 2⅞ yards, each	1.50 to	. . . .	1.88
4430	2½ x 2¾ yards, each	1.28 to	. . . .	1.75

Extra Length Hemstitched Sheets

4431	1¾ yards wide, each	$1.15 to	. . . . .	$1.66
4432	2 yards wide, each	1.25 to	. . . .	1.95
4433	2¼ yards wide, each	1.35 to	. . . .	1.98
4434	2½ yards wide, each	1.45 to	. . . .	2.05
4435	2¾ yards wide, each	1.88 to	. . . .	2.24

Miscellaneous

4436	Absorbent Cotton, ½-pound packages, each	. . . . . .	$ .18
4437	Absorbent Cotton, 1-pound packages, each	. . . . . .	.35
4438	Sterilized Gauze, in box, 12-yard lengths, each	. . . .	.65
4439	Lamb's Wool Wadding, 17 x 38 inches	. . . . .	.20
4440	Lamb's Wool, comfortable size, 72 x 84 inches .	. . . .	2.10

Scalloped Sheets and Pillow Cases

4441	Plain hem, 72 x 108 inches, each, $1.50; hemstitched, each		$1.65
4442	Plain hem, 90 x 108 inches, each, $1.65; hemstitched, each	.	1.75

Scalloped Pillow Cases, to match plain hem

4443	According to size, each, 40c., 45c. and	. . . . .	$ .50

Scalloped Pillow Cases, to match hemstitched

4444	According to size, each, 45c., 55c. and	. . . . .	$ .65

Sizes quoted indicate length before hemming

FLOOR COVERINGS ADAPTED FOR SPRING AND SUMMER USE

In the American Rug Department an extensive assortment of moderately priced Spring and Summer Floor Coverings is maintained. Attention is directed to a variety of fabrics and color designs suitable for use with Chints, or Cretonne draperies. In addition to rugs of this character, a rug in solid plain colors is specially featured and which can be furnished (within three days) in nine different shades and in any width not exceeding fifteen feet.

A large and varied collection of weatherproof floor coverings is shown, especially adapted to verandas, sun parlors, house boats and yachts.

ORIENTAL RUGS

The assortment of Oriental Rugs is one of the largest and most interesting ever brought to America. These rugs were separately selected by B. Altman & Co's New York buyers on an extended trip through the Orient and into the interior of Persia and the Caucasus. All inferior qualities were eliminated and only the class of merchandise adapted to American requirements was accepted. The wearing qualities of all Rugs are fully guaranteed by B. Altman & Co.

ART OBJECTS AND BRIC-A-BRAC

4501 Brass Smoking Stand, with two cigar rests, match holder and glass tray; special, at $1.35
4502 Oval Mirror, of gilt wood, with easel back; 10 x 12 inches; special, at 3.00

4503 Pedestal Picture Frame, of gilt wood, square or oval; 8 x 10 inches $3.75
4504 Mahogany Book Blocks, with marquetry inlay, pair . . . 4.00
4505 Solid Mahogany Electric Lamp, with two lights; height, 26 inches; 13-inch silk shade, in écru, rose or green; effective gold shell trimming medallions of French print and 4-inch silk fringe 12.50
4506 Metal Standard Electric Lamp, brush brass or Japanese bronze finish; height, 13 inches; with silk shade in écru, rose or green 3.75
4507 Mahogany Candlestick, with glass bobache; height, 10 inches; special, at 1.85
4508 Silvered or Brass Metal Shade, with linen lining, mica lined; in rose, yellow, white or red; bugle and bell fringe . . 1.25
4508A Silvered or Brass Metal Shade only 40
4508B Linen Lining for the above, with bugle and bell fringe, mica lined, 85c.; with plain bugle fringe, 75c.; with seed-bead fringe 40
4509 Portable Electric Lamp, nickel finish, with 12-foot cord, stands, hangs or clamps; may be adjusted to any angle, and has rubber suction cup for securely fastening lamp to mirror or any non-porous surface 2.00
4510 Adjustable Floor Lamp, with goose-neck; brush brass finish; metal shade (*not illustrated*) 4.75
4511 Silver-plated Candlestick, 8 inches high (*not illustrated*) . 1.45

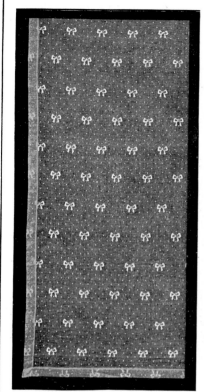

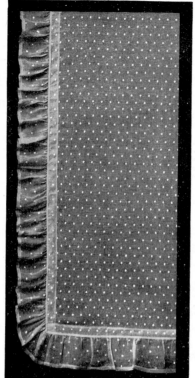

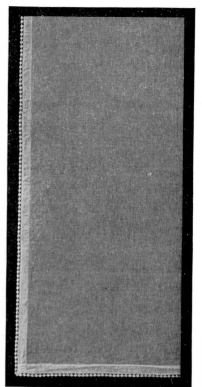

4601 Figured Muslin Curtains, plain
hemstitched edge, white only, 34
inches wide, 2½ yards long, per pair $1.25
4601A Same, 3 yards long, per pair . . . 1.50

4602 Hemstitched Ruffled Muslin Curtains, with hemstitched band in
curtains, white only, 38 inches wide,
2½ yards long, per pair $1.15
4602A Same, 3 yards long, per pair . . . 1.35

4603 Hemstitched Scrim Curtains, trimmed with edge, white or écru, 32
inches wide, 2½ yards long, per
pair $1.00

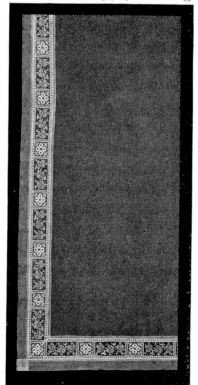

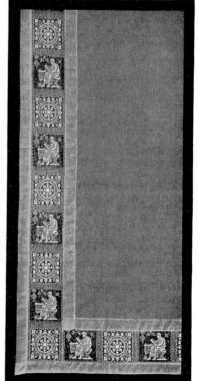

4604 Cable Net Curtains, trimmed with
novelty beading and braid edge,
white or écru, 32 inches wide, 2½
yards long, per pair $1.35

4605 Cable Net Curtains, imitation filet
lace, plain hemmed edge, white or
écru, 34 inches wide, 2½ yards long,
per pair $1.35

4606 Hemstitched Scrim Curtains, with
imitation filet lace, hemmed edge,
white or écru, 38 inches wide, 2½
yards long, per pair $2.75
4606A Same style, 3 yards long, per pair . 3.25

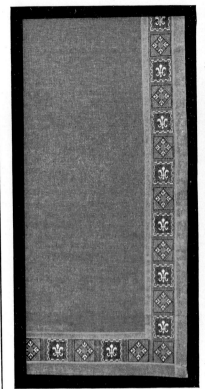

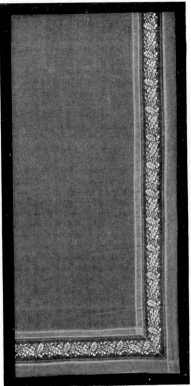

4607 Hemstitched Scrim Curtains, with imitation filet lace, hemmed edge, white or écru, 36 inches wide, 2½ yards long, per pair $1.35

4608 Hemstitched Scrim Curtains, imitation filet lace, plain hemmed edge, white or écru, 37 in. x 2½ yds., pair $1.95
4608A Same, 3 yards long, per pair . . 2.25

4609 Marie Antoinette and Embroidered Lace Curtains, mounted on extra quality cable net, white or écru, 38 inches wide, 3 yards long, per pair $3.25

UPHOLSTERY AND DRAPERY DEPARTMENT

In this Department will be found complete assortments of fabrics in all weights and textures suitable for Hangings, Draperies, Wall Coverings and various Upholstery purposes. Samples and complete information furnished upon request

WASHABLE CURTAIN FABRICS

4701 Lappet Muslin, dot and figured, 39 inches wide, yard $ .17
4702 Scotch Muslin, dot, floral, art nouveau and colonial patterns, 36 inches wide, yard, 27c. to 40c.; 45 inches wide, yard, 32c. to 65
4703 Embroidered Swiss Muslin, scalloped edges, 30 and 36 inches wide, yard, 29c. to 75
4704 Dotted Swiss Muslin, plain edges, 30 and 40 inches wide, yard, 35c. to 1.10
4705 Tamboured Muslin, for sash curtains, 28 inches wide, yard, 25c. to 50c.; 36 inches wide, yard, 55c. and . . .60
4706 Tamboured Muslin, for long curtains, 48 in. wide, yard .75
4707 Ruffled Swiss Muslin, plain body, scalloped dotted ruffle, 30 inches wide, yard 30
4708 Ruffled Swiss Muslin, all-over dotted, scalloped edge, 30 inches wide, yard, 38c.; 40 inches wide, yard, 65c.; 50 inches wide, yard 75
4709 White Dotted Grenadine, 49 inches wide, yard 58
4710 Plain Scrim and Marquisette, white, cream and écru, 38 to 48 inches wide, yard, 18c. to 50
4711 Blocked Scrim, corded and drawn, white, cream and écru, 38 inches wide, yard, 22c. to 60
4712 Hemstitched Bordered Scrim and Marquisette, white, ivory and écru, 38 inches wide, yard 35
4713 French Etamine, plain, 42 inches wide, yard, 60c. to 1.25
4714 French Linen Scrim, 50 inches wide, yard 1.25
4715 French Etamine, 1½ to 8-inch drawn blocks, 42 to 48 inches wide, yard, 60c. to 3.00
4716 Fancy Fish Net, 38 to 50 inches wide, yard, 15c. to . .60
4717 English and Scotch Novelty Net, 42 to 54 inches wide, yard, 40c. to 1.50
4718 Figured Filet Net, in symmetrical and mythological figures, 45 to 54 inches wide, yard, 55c. to 2.45
4719 Plain Filet Net, white, ivory or écru, 45 inches wide, yard, 28c. to 50

4720 Imported Bobbinets, white, ivory or écru, in a wide range of meshes, 54, 80, 90, 108 and 126 inches wide, priced according to width and quality, yard, 40c. to . $2.00
4721 Point d'Esprit Net, fine quality, white and cream, 72 inches wide, yard 85
4722 French Batiste, cream, 50 inches wide, yard 50

DRAPERY SILKS AND MADRAS

4723 Japanese Silks, a large range of plain colors, 30 inches wide, yard, 65c.; 36 inches wide, yard . . . . . $ .80
4724 Figured Japanese and Corean Silks, floral designs, 31 inches wide, yard, 60c. and 75
4725 Royal Silk, rich, soft drapery fabric, plain, 50 inches wide, $1.75; with small self figure, 50 inches wide 1.95
4726 Figured Nara Yama Silk, cream and colored grounds, chintz patterns, 31 and 33 inches wide, yard 1.25
4727 Silk and Wool English Casement Cloth, in plain and self-figured ivory, cream and écru, 50 inches wide, yard 1.60
4728 Plain Mercerized English Casement Cloth, in écru only, 50 inches wide, yard, 85c. and 1.50
4729 White or Écru Madras, 30 to 52 inches wide, yard, 25c. to .95
4730 Complete Line of Scotch Madras, white ground with color combinations, of light blue, dark blue, pink, green, lavender, rose, yellow or brown, 30 to 50 inches wide, yard, 65c. to $1.95; dark grounds, in suitable color combinations, 30, 40 and 50 inches wide, yard, 65c., 75c. 1.25
4731 Plain Sun-fast Light Weight Mercerized Poplin, in a variety of popular colors, 50 inches wide, yard 85
4732 Plain Sun-fast Corean Silk, in complete line of colors, 30 inches wide, yard 75
4733 Kapock Silk, a highly lustrous light weight drapery fabric, in range of plain colors, 50 inches wide, yard . 1.60
4734 Figured Pongee Silk, 28 inches wide, yard 1.25

UPHOLSTERY AND DRAPERY DEPARTMENT—(Continued)

CRETONNES, LINENS AND TAFFETAS

A large assortment, including English and French prints, offers many exclusive designs at moderate prices

4735	Imported Cretonnes, 31 in. wide, yard, 35c., 45c., 50c. to	$1.50
4736	Figured Linen Taffeta, 50 inches wide, yard, $1.50 to	3.75
4737	Reversible Shadow Taffeta, 50 inches wide, yard, $1.50 to $4.25; 31 inches wide, yard, 60c. and	.95
4738	Plain Linens, 50 inches wide, in all colors, yard	1.00
4739	Jacquard Linen, for slip covers, 50 inches wide, yard	.70
4740	White Figured English Dimity, for bedspreads, 31 inches wide, yard, 50c.; 50 inches wide, yard, $1.00; 65 inches wide, yard, $1.25 ; plain stripe, 31 inches wide, yard	.48
4741	Valance Dimity, 22 inches wide, yard	.38
4742	Plain Sateens, for lining draperies and spreads, in all the desirable shades, 50 inches wide; domestic, yard, 23c.; imported, yard	.75
4743	Linen Taffeta, plain colors, 50 inches wide, yard	.60
4744	Hand Block and Printed Linens, including cubist and futurist designs, 31 inches wide, yard, $1.25 and $2.75 ; 50 inches wide, yard, $3.00 to	3.50
4745	Cotton and Mercerized Cotton Jaspe Cloth, all colors, 50 inches wide, yard, 95c. to	1.35

DOMESTIC PRINTS

4746	Figured Chintz, 33 and 36 inches wide, yard, 18c. to	$ .45
4747	Plain Art Ticking, 36 inches wide, yard	.24
4748	Figured Art Ticking, 33 and 36 inches wide, yard, 28c. to	.35
4749	Plain Taffeta, 36 inches wide, yard	.28
4750	Figured Taffeta, in floral and shaded designs; 36 inches wide, yard, 32c. and	.35
4751	Figured Jute Taffeta, 36 inches wide, yard, 48c. to	.60
4752	Plain Real Denim, 36 inches wide, yard	.25
4753	Self-figured Plain Colored Denim, 36 inches wide, yard, 32c. and	.40
4754	Pongee Silkoline, plain colors, 36 inches wide, yard	.10
4755	Pongee Silkoline, figured, 36 inches wide, yard	.12
4756	Imported Japanese Crepe, figured, 30 inches wide, yard	.25
4757	Serpentine Crepe, floral designs, 29 inches wide, yard	.18
4758	Plain Dimity, all colors, 36 inches wide, yard	.24
4759	Homespun, plain colors, 40 inches wide, yard	.35
4760	Shadow and Floral Rep Cretonnes, yard, 38c. to	.45
4761	Figured Sateen, yard, 25c. and	.35
4762	Figured Nainsilk, floral effects; suitable for quilt and comfortable coverings; 36 inches wide, yard	.28

FRINGES, GALLOONS, ETC.

4763	Cotton Ball Fringe, chintz and plain colors, yard, 5c. and	$ .08
4764	Cotton Tassel Fringe, chintz colors, yard, 6c. and	.08
4765	Cotton Edges and Cut Fringes, chintz colorings, 3c. to	.16
4766	Silk Edges, cut, also uncut, yard, 15c., 32c. to	.85
4767	Silk Tassel Fringe, various colors, 12c., 15c. to	.85
4768	Silk Lamp Shade Fringe, 2 and 4 inches wide, large assortment of colors, yard, 50c. and	.75
4769	Imported French Trimmings, floral effects, suitable for lamp shades and fancy work, yard, 30c. to	1.50

FRINGES, GALLOONS, ETC. (Continued)

4770	Silk Serpentine Gimp, ⅜ inch wide, to match lamp shade fringes, yard	$ .12
4771	Cotton and Silk Pillow Cords, yard, 8c., 12c. and	.32
4772	Silk Pillow Girdles, 3 yards long, with tassels, each, 50c. and	.60
4773	Mercerized Pillow Girdles, 3 yards long, with tassel at each end	.24
4774	White Cotton Bedspread Fringes, yard, 12c. to	.24
4775	Linen Fringes for Scarfs, natural color, brown and cream, 3 to 4 inches wide, yard, 18c. to	.40
4776	Sun-fast Cut Fringe, single and double beadings, large assortment of colors, yard, 9c. and	.15
4777	Furniture Cord, yard	.06
4778	Furniture Gimp, yard, 4c. and	.07
4779	Silk Loops, pair, 25c. to	1.75
4780	Cotton Loops, white, cream or écru, pair, 8c. to	.40
4781	Portière Bindings, double-edge mercerized cotton, various colors, yard	.15
4782	Metal Antique Galloons, gold or silver, ¼ to 4 inches wide, large variety of patterns, yard, 8c. to	.85
4783	Metal Antique Fringes, gold or silver, yard, 18c. to	1.50
4784	Metal Antique Lace, gold or silver, yard, 25c., 35c. and	.50
4785	Gold or Silver Tassels, each 15c. to	.35
4786	Gold or Silver Cords, yard, 8c. to	.32
4787	**Domestic Holland Window Shades**, mounted on wood, spring rollers, ready to be put up, 3 x 6 feet, in white, écru, moss green and dark green, each	.45
4788	**Sun-fast Domestic Holland Window Shades**, 3 x 6 feet, in white, each, 60c.; melrose, 70c.; olive green and dark green	.75

Imported Taffeta Bedspreads and Table Covers, in vari-colored floral designs.

Couch Hammocks with Windshield, of heavy quality canvas; with best springs and denim-covered mattresses; colors, green, khaki and white; with or without Iron Frame Stands and Canopies.

Cedar Chests, also Utility Boxes, covered with matting or cretonne.

Screens, of mahogany, fumed oak or white enamel, paneled with appropriate materials; also Embroidered Japanese Screens.

Foot Stools, in mahogany and oak; covered with tapestry.

King's Scotch Holland Shades, made to measurements.

When ordering, give exact width and length of window casing, and whether inside or outside fixtures are required. Samples and estimates furnished.

Complete Department of White Enamel and Nickel Bathroom Fixtures.

Dark Green Porch Shades, sizes from 4 ft. to 12 ft. wide by 7 ft. 8 in. long, at moderate prices.

"SUN-FAST" (NON-FADEABLE) DRAPERY AND UPHOLSTERY FABRICS

PLAIN AND FIGURED MATERIALS (BY THE YARD)

4789	Sun-fast Madras, white grounds in dainty designs and combinations of light blue, pink, yellow, green and lavender, all-over patterns, 40 inches wide, yard, 60c.; 50 inches wide, yard, 95c., $1.25 and	$2.45
4789A	Same color combinations bordered on both sides, 36 inches wide, yard, 60c.; 46 inches wide, yard	.75
4790	Sun-fast Light Weight Drapery Fabrics, in all desirable plain colors, 32 inches wide, yard, 55c.; 36 inches wide, yard, 50c., 55c. and 58c.; 50 inches wide, yard, 85c. and	.95
4791	Sun-fast Self-figured Colored Madras, in a wide range of desirable colors, 50 inches wide, yard, 95c. and	1.25
4792	Plain Rough Finish Sun-fast Shiki Silk, in a variety of plain colors, 31 inches wide, yard	1.10
4793	Sun-fast Double-faced Mercerized Poplin, in colors to	

	match any color scheme or combination, 50 inches wide, yard, 95c. and	$1.25
4794	Sun-fast Double-faced Fancy Rep and Shiki, very attractive colors, 50 inches wide, yard, $1.10 and	1.50
4795	Sun-fast, Light Weight Armure, very attractive designs and colorings ; 50 inches wide, yard, $1.35, $1.65 and	2.25
4796	Sun-fast, Double-faced Armure, plain colors, 50 inches wide, yard, $1.35, $1.65 and	2.00
4797	Sun-fast Tapestry, small pattern, 50 inches wide, yard, $2.00 and	2.25

SUN-FAST CURTAINS AND PORTIÈRES (MADE UP)

4798	Light Weight Semi-transparent Sun-fast, with floral and conventional patterns, in two-tone greens, browns, reds, blues and rose ; 2½ yards long, at $3.00, $3.50, $4.00, $4.50, $5.00, $5.50, $6.00, $6.50 and	$7.25

LINEN DEPARTMENT

4901 Fine Madeira Hand-scalloped Afternoon Tea Napkins, one corner ornamented with Madeira eyelet embroidery ; size, 14 x 14 inches, per dozen $5.25

4902 Fine Plain Irish Linen Hemstitched Afternoon Tea Napkins, mitred corners ; size, 15 x 15 inches, per dozen 3.25

4903 Double Satin Damask Afternoon Tea Napkins, hemstitched ; size, 15 x 15 inches, per dozen 5.00

4904 Fine Hand-made French Cluny Lace Tumbler Doylies, Plate Doylies and Centerpieces. Doylies, size, 6 inches, each, 25c.; size, 12 inches, each, 75c. Centerpieces, size, 28 inches, each 3.90

4905 Fine Hemstitched Damask Afternoon Tea Napkins ; size, 15 x 15 inches, per dozen 4.25

4906 Fine Hand-scalloped Luncheon Sets, of Madeira eyelet embroidery ; comprising six tumbler doylies, six plate doylies and one 24-inch centerpiece ; the set of thirteen pieces . . . 8.50

4907 Hemstitched and Hand-embroidered Irish Linen Dresser Scarfs ; size, 18 x 54 inches, each 1.25

4907A Pillow Shams, to match No. 4907 ; size, 30 x 30 inches, per pair $2.50

4908 Madeira Hand-scalloped and Embroidered Luncheon Sets ; comprising six tumbler doylies, six plate doylies and one 24-inch centerpiece ; the set of thirteen pieces 4.50

4909 Fine Double Satin Damask Machine-scalloped Round Table Cloths ; size, 72 inches, each, $6.00 ; size, 80 inches, each, $7.50 ; size, 90 inches, each, $9.00. Napkins to match, square ; size, 25 x 25 inches, per dozen 10.50

4910 Double Satin Damask Afternoon Tea Napkins, hemstitched, assorted designs ; size, 15 x 15 inches, per dozen 5.00

4911 Hemstitched Damask Afternoon Tea Napkins ; size, 15 x 15 inches, per dozen 2.40

4912 Fine Madeira Hand-scalloped Afternoon Tea Napkins ; size, 14 x 14 inches, per dozen 4.75

4913 Fine Hemstitched Damask Afternoon Tea Cloths ; size, 45 x 45 inches, each, $1.80 ; size, 54 x 54 inches, each 2.50

4914 Fine Hemstitched Damask Afternoon Tea Napkins, to match No. 4913; size, 15 x 15 inches, per dozen 3.00

4950

4951

4952

4953

4954

LINEN DAMASK TABLE CLOTHS, NAPKINS, ETC.

In the Linen Department a very large assortment of patterns and sizes of Linen Damask Table Cloths and Napkins is maintained in stock, representing the productions of the most reliable manufacturers of Ireland, France, Germany, Belgium and Scotland; also a carefully selected variety of Decorative Linens, Bed Linens, Towels and Towelings. Particular attention is given to the furnishing of Household Linens for Bridal Outfits, and to the Embroidering of Crests, Monograms or Initials. A special feature is made of Linens with names, monograms or crests woven in, for Hotels, Clubs, Restaurants and Institutions. Designs, samples and estimates will be submitted upon application.

4950 Heavy Double Damask Table Cloths, circular design; will be supplied square or cut round upon request; size, 2 x 2 yards, each, $3.75; 2¼ x 2¼ yards, each, $5.25; 2½ x 2½ yards, each, $6.50. Dinner Napkins to match, per dozen $5.25

4951 Heavy Double Satin Damask Table Cloths; size, 2 x 2 yards, each, $4.00; 2 x 2½ yards, each, $5.00; 2 x 3 yards, each, $6.00; 2¼ x 2¼ yards, each, $5.25. Dinner Napkins to match, per dozen 5.50

4952 Heavy Bleached Irish Damask Table Cloths, excellent wearing quality; assorted designs; size, 70 x 70 inches, each, $2.25; 70 x 87 inches, each, $2.85. Napkins to match, breakfast size, per dozen, $2.25; dinner size, per dozen . 3.25

4953 Fine Double Satin Damask Table Cloths, circular design; will be supplied square or cut round upon request; size, 2 x 2 yards, each, $4.50; 2¼ x 2¼ yards, each, $6.25; 2½ x 2½ yards, each, $7.50. Dinner Napkins to match, per dozen 6.90

4954 Very Fine Double Satin Damask Table Cloths, circular design ; will be supplied square or cut round upon request; size, 2 x 2 yards, each, $5.40; 2¼ x 2¼ yards, each, $7.25; 2½ x 2½ yards, each, $9.00. Napkins to match, breakfast size, per dozen, $6.25; dinner size, per dozen 8.50

The Round Table Cloths illustrated can also be supplied cut square. Those illustrated cut square can only be supplied as shown. In ordering numbers that can be furnished either round or square, please state which is desired.

NOTE—The prices quoted for the Bordered Table Cloths Illustrated are the same as for damask of equal quality—purchased by the yard.

Not Illustrated

4955 Very Heavy Double Satin Damask Table Cloths, assorted designs, suitable for round, square or oblong tables; size, 2 x 2 yards, each, $4.75; 2 x 2½ yards, each, $6.00; 2 x 3 yards, each, $7.00; 2 x 3½ yards, each, $8.25; 2 x 4 yards, each, $9.25; 2¼ x 2¼ yards, each, $6.50; 2½ x 2½ yards, each, $8.25; 2½ x 3 yards, each, $9.75; 2½ x 3½ yards, each, $11.50; 2½ x 4 yards, each, $13.00. Dinner Napkins to match, per dozen $7.50

4956 Very Heavy Double Damask Table Cloths, choice assortment of designs; suitable for round, square or oblong tables; size, 2 x 2 yards, each, $4.00; 2 x 2½ yards, each, $5.00; 2 x 3 yards, each, $6.25; 2 x 3½ yards, each, $7.00; 2 x 4 yards, each, $8.25; 2¼ x 2¼ yards, each, $5.75; 2½ x 2½ yards, each, $7.00; 2½ x 3 yards, each, $8.50; 2½ x 3½ yards, each, $10.00; 2½ x 4 yards, each, $11.50. Dinner Napkins to match, per dozen . . . 6.50

4957 Very Fine Double Satin Damask Table Cloths, a large assortment of new designs ; size, 2 x 2 yards, each, $7.00 ; 2 x 2½ yards, each, $8.75 ; 2 x 3 yards, each, $10.50 ; 2 x 3½ yards, each, $12.50 ; 2 x 4 yards, each, $14.00 ; 2¼ x 2¼ yards, each, $9.50 ; 2½ x 2½ yards, each, $11.50 ; 2½ x 3 yards, each, $14.00 ; 2½ x 3½ yards, each, $16.50 ; 2½ x 4 yards, each, $19.00. Dinner Napkins to match, per dozen 9.75

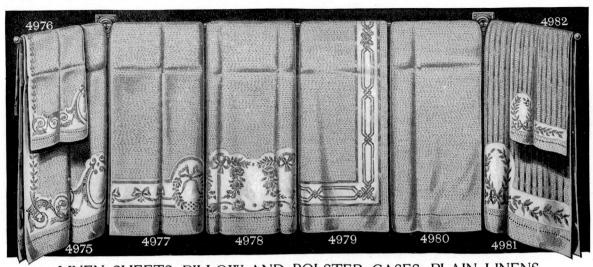

LINEN SHEETS, PILLOW AND BOLSTER CASES, PLAIN LINENS SHEETINGS, ETC.

TOWELS

4975 Fine Quality Hemstitched Huck Towels, damask side and end borders, suitable for monogram; white only; size, 22 x 40 inches, per dozen $7.75

4976 Guests' Towels, of fine hemstitched linen huckaback, damask side and end borders, suitable for monogram; white only; size, 14 x 22 inches, per dozen 3.00

4977 Fine Soft-finished Hemstitched Huck Towels, all linen, excellent wearing quality, damask end borders, suitable for monogram; white only; size, 22 x 40 inches, per dozen 4.20

4978 Soft-finished Hemstitched Huck Towels, all linen, assorted damask end borders; white only; size, 20 x 38 inches, per dozen 3.00

4979 Fine Soft-finished Hemstitched Huck Towels, damask end and side borders; white only; size, 21 x 38 inches, per dozen . 6.00

4980 Soft-finished Irish Linen Hemstitched Huck Towels, especially made for cross-stitch embroidery; white only; size 22 x 38 inches, per dozen, $5.50; size, 24 x 40 inches, per dozen . . . 6.50

4981 Fine Quality Hemstitched Huck Towels, stripe center, damask end borders, suitable for monogram; white only; size, 22 x 38 inches, per dozen 6.00

4982 Guests' Hemstitched Towels, striped huck center, damask end borders, suitable for monogram; white only; size, 16 x 24 inches, per dozen 4.00

LINEN DAMASK TABLE CLOTHS NAPKINS, ETC.— (Continued)

Not Illustrated

4958 Extra Large Damask Dinner Cloths are regularly maintained in stock; sizes, 3 x 3 yards, 3½ x 3½ yards, 4 x 4 yards, 5 x 5 yards; prices and descriptions on application.

4959 Linen Damask Table Napkins; size, 17 x 17 inches, per dozen, $1.00, $1.25; 19 x 19 inches, per dozen, $1.50, $1.90; 20 x 20 inches, per dozen, $2.00, $2.50, $3.00, $3.75; 24 x 24 inches, per dozen, $2.00, $2.50, $3.00, $3.75 to $6.00; 26 x 26 inches, per dozen, $4.75, $5.50 to $7.00; 27 x 27 inches, per dozen, $5.50, $7.50, $9.00 to $27.50

4960 Fine Damask Hemstitched Afternoon Tea Cloths; size, 36 x 36 inches, each, $1.25, $1.50, $2.00 and $3.00; 44 x 44 inches, each, $1.75, $2.50, $3.25 and $4.00; 54 x 54 inches, each, $2.50, $3.00, $3.75 and 6.00

4961 Hemstitched Linen Tea Cloths; size, 36 x 36 inches, each, $1.00 and $1.25; 45 x 45 inches, each, $1.25 and 1.50

4962 Hemstitiched and Hand-embroidered Pillow Shams; size, 32 x 32 inches, per pair, $2.50, $2.90, $3.50 to 9.00

LINEN SHEETS, PILLOW AND BOLSTER CASES, ETC.—Not Illustrated

4983 Hemstitched Linen Sheets, for single beds; size, 72 x 90 inches, per pair, $3.50, $4.25; 72 x 96 inches, per pair, $4.00, $5.00, $6.00, $7.50; 72 x 108 inches, per pair, $7.25, $9.00, $10.50 to . . $15.00

4984 Hemstitched Linen Sheets, for double beds; size, 90 x 96 inches, per pair, $4.75, $6.00, $7.00, $8.00, $9.00; 90 x 108 inches, per pair, $7.50, $9.50, $13.50 to 20.00

4985 Hemstitched Linen Pillow Cases; size, 22½ x 36 inches, per pair, $1.00, $1.25, $1.50, $2.00 to $3.00

4986 Hemstitched Linen Pillow Cases; size, 25 x 36 inches, per pair, $1.50, $1.75, $2.25 to 3.25

4987 Hemstitched Linen Pillow Cases; size, 27 x 36 inches, per pair, $1.60, $2.00, $2.50 to 3.50

4988 Hemstitched Linen Bolster Cases, for single beds; size, 21 x 54 inches, each, 90c., $1.20, $1.50 to 1.90

4989 Hemstitched Linen Bolster Cases, for double beds; size, 21 x 72 inches, each, $1.00, $1.25, $1.50, $2.00, $2.40 to 2.90

4990 Bleached Irish Linens, for pillow and bolster cases; 40 inches wide, yard, 50c., 65c., 75c.; 42 inches wide, 60c., 75c., 85c.; 45 inches wide, 65c., 80c., 90c.; 50 inches wide, 70c., 80c., $1.00; 54 inches wide, 80c., $1.00 . . . . 1.10

4991 Bleached Linen Sheeting; 72 inches wide, yard, 70c., 90c., $1.10, $1.25, $1.50; 90 inches wide, 90c., $1.10, $1.25, $1.50 . 1.75

4992 Bleached Irish Linens, medium weights; 36 inches wide, yard, 35c., 50c., 65c., 75c. 1.00

4993 Bleached Irish Linens, heavy weight; 36 inches wide, yard, 50c., 75c., $1.00 . . . . 1.25

4994 Soft Finish Linens; 36 inches wide, yard, 40c., 50c. 60

4995 Hemstitched and Hand-embroidered Sheer Lawn Bedspreads, for single beds; size, 72 x 108 inches, each, $8.00, $9.50, $12.00, $13.50 . . . . 16.50

4996 Hemstitched and Hand-embroidered Sheer Lawn Bedspreads, for double beds; size, 90 x 108 inches, each, $9.00, $10.50, $12.00, $13.50, $15.00 and 18.50

4997 Hemmed Huck Towels, per dozen, $1.25, $1.50, $1.75, $2.00, $3.00, $3.50 to 6.00

4998 Hemstitched Huck Towels, per dozen, $2.00, $2.50, $3.00, $4.50, $5.00, $6.00, $7.50, $9.00 to 20.00

4999 Hemstitched Damask Towels, per dozen, $3.00, $4.50, $6.00 to 12.00

5000 White Turkish Bath Towels, per dozen, $1.50, $2.00, $2.50, $3.00, $4.50, $6.00, $7.50 to 18.00

5001 Brown Linen Turkish Bath Towels, each, 50c., 60c., 75c., to . 1.50

5002 Turkish Bath Sheets, each, $1.00, $1.50, $2.00, $2.50, $3.50 to 5.00

5003 Linen Diapering, per piece of ten yards; 18 inches, $1.25, $1.40, $1.75, $2.25, $2.75; 20 inches, $1.40, $1.60, $2.00, $2.40, $3.00; 22 inches, $1.75, $2.25, $2.90, $3.25; 24 inches, $2.25, $2.75, $3.50; 26 inches, $2.50, $3.00 . . . . 3.75

5004 Cotton Diapering, soft finished, per piece of ten yards; 18 inches, 55c., 85c.; 20 inches, 60c., 92c.; 22 inches, 65c., $1.00; 24 inches, 70c., $1.05; 27 inches, 80c. 1.15

5005 Rubber Sheeting, per yard; 27 inches, 35c.; 36 inches, 48c.; 45 inches, 75c.; 54 inches 80

5006 Rubber Sheets, each; size, 1¼ x 2 yards, $2.50; 2 x 2 yards . 3.40

5007 Hemmed Turkish Wash Cloths, each, 5c., 7c., 10c. to 20

5008 Sponge or Dish Cloths, each, 5c., 8c. and 10

5009 Paint Cloths, each, 5c., 8c., 10c. and 12

5010 Floor Cloths, each, 5c., 8c., 10c., 12c. to 25

NOTE—Prices of Cotton Diapering, also Rubber Sheets and Sheeting, are subject to change

5101
5102
5120
5103
5104
5105
5106
5107
5108
5122
5116
5117
5121
5115
5118
5119
5109
5110
5111
5112
5113
5114

For prices and descriptions, see page 75

DISTINCTIVE FOOTWEAR FOR WOMEN

Practically every demand of the Boot, Shoe and Slipper is covered in the illustrated list taken from the large and complete assortment in vogue for Spring and Summer. Unusual care has been taken in the selection of the materials, workmanship and fitting qualities of the lasts employed. Slipper Trimmings are especially featured, a department being maintained for supplying the newest and most favored in Garnitures. This is the pre-eminent season of the Sports Shoe, those for Tennis, Golf, Boating and Outing appearing in new and privileged smartness. Complete assortments of every footwear appeal are constantly maintained, or any style carefully executed to special requirements.

5101	Women's Pumps, in black gun-metal or tan calfskin, patent leather or white canvas; welt soles and 1⅞-inch leather heels	$5.00
5101A	Similar style, in patent leather or black gun-metal calf, with 1⅜-inch leather heels . . .	5.00
5102	Women's Evening Ties, in bronze or dull kid, patent leather or white calf	5.00
5103	Women's Kid Boudoir Slippers, in black, red or tan, also Himalaya cloth; in light blue or pink, with silk pompons; medium width only; with heels, $1.25; without heels . . .	.95
5104	**Women's Oxfords, in black gun-metal or tan calf, with heavy soles, and low heels, suitable for walking; at the special price of** . . .	5.00
5105	Women's Oxford Ties, in black gun-metal or tan calf, or patent leather, with welt soles and 1⅞-inch heels, $5.00; in black kid, without perforations, welt soles and 1¾-inch heels, $5.00; black kid, with turn soles	5.00
5105A	Women's White Buckskin Oxford Ties, welt soles, 1⅞-inch heels	6.00
5106	Women's Button or Lace Boots, in black gun-metal or tan calfskin	5.00
5107	Women's Tramping or Golf Boots, in black calfskin or tan oilgrain; 1½-inch broad military heels and heavy welt soles	6.00
5108	Women's Colonial Ties, in black gun-metal or tan calf, patent leather or white canvas; welt soles and 1⅞-inch leather heels	5.00
5109	Women's Brocade Boudoir Slippers, in light blue or pink, also plain black satin, with dressy chiffon rosettes; sizes, 3 to 7; B and D width (no half sizes)	2.00
5110	Women's Oxford Ties, in black gun-metal calf, white buckskin quarter, with black gun-metal vamp; or white buckskin quarter with patent leather vamp; light weight welt soles, leather heels	6.00
5111	Women's Dressy Afternoon Pumps, black gun-metal or patent leather quarter with white calf vamp, turn soles and covered wood heels to match vamp	8.00
5112	Women's Novelty Oxfords, with light-weight welted soles and leather heels, in patent coltskin, black or mahogany tan calfskin	6.00
5112A	Same as above, white buckskin, with white soles and covered wood heels, $8.00; white buckskin quarter and white calf vamp	8.00
5113	Women's Evening Slippers, in black, white, pink or blue satin; bronze or dull kid, patent leather or white calf	5.00
5114	Women's Novelty Pumps, with gray buckskin quarter and patent leather vamp; gray buckskin quarter and black gun-metal vamp; champagne buckskin quarter and black gun-metal vamp; or champagne buckskin quarter and patent leather vamp; covered wood heels and light-weight welt soles	7.00
5115	Women's White Buckskin Colonial Ties, light weight welt soles and 1⅞-inch covered wood heels	$6.00
5115A	Women's Light Weight Colonial Ties, in patent leather or black gun-metal calf, with turn soles and 1⅞-inch covered wood heels	5.00
5116	Women's Tennis Boots, with rubber soles and leather toe pieces; white buckskin, $7.00; tan calfskin	5.00
5117	Women's White Buckskin Golf Boots, rubber soles and heels, leather toe pieces	7.00
5118	Women's Golf Boots, of tan calfskin, rubber soles and heels, leather toe pieces	7.00
5119	Women's Tennis Oxfords, with rubber soles and leather toe pieces; white buckskin, $6.00; tan calfskin	4.00

MISSES' AND CHILDREN'S FOOTWEAR

Children's Shoes up to size 11½ have spring heels. First heels appear only in larger sizes

CORRECT SHAPES FOR THE YOUTHFUL FOOT

5120	Misses' Shoes; sizes, 11 to 2, patent leather, button, $3.00; black gun-metal or tan calfskin, button or lace, $3.00; white buckskin, button, $4.00; white canvas	$2.50
5121	Young Ladies' Shoes; sizes, 2½ to 5½, 1¼-inch heels, patent leather, button, $3.50; tan calfskin or black gun-metal calf, button or lace, $3.50; white buckskin, button, $6.00; white canvas, button	3.50
5122	Children's Shoes; sizes, 8 to 10½, patent leather, button, $2.50; black gun-metal or tan calf, button or lace, $2.50; white buckskin, button, $3.50; white canvas	2.00
5123	Patent Leather Slippers; sizes, 7 to 10½, $2.00; 11 to 2, $2.50; 2½ to 5½	3.25
5123A	White Kid Slippers; sizes, 11 to 2, $2.50; 2½ to 5½	3.25
5124	Young Women's Pumps; sizes, 2½ to 5½; tan calfskin, black gun-metal calfskin or patent leather, $3.50; white buckskin, $4.00; white canvas	3.00
5125	Tan or Black Kid Ankle Ties; sizes, 2 to 6, 85c.; white buckskin	1.50
5126	Children's Felt Slippers, with rabbit design; in red, navy, light blue or pink; sizes, 6 to 2 . .	.90
5127	Infants' Button Shoes; sizes, 2 to 6, black kid, $1.10; tan calfskin, $1.25; white buckskin . .	1.75
5128	Children's Button Shoes; sizes, 4 to 8, tan calfskin or black gun-metal calfskin, $1.75; white buckskin, $2.50; white canvas	1.35
5129	Ankle Ties, tan calfskin or black gun-metal calf; sizes, 4 to 8, $1.50; 8½ to 10½, $2.00; 11 to 2	2.50
5129A	Ankle Ties, white buckskin; sizes, 4 to 8, $2.00; 8½ to 10½, $2.50; 11 to 2	3.50
5129B	Ankle Ties, patent leather; sizes, 4 to 8, $1.75; 8½ to 10½, $2.25; 11 to 2	2.75

HOSIERY

The subject of Hosiery grows more interesting and comprehensive with each season, new styles and weights making added appeal; and for the many individual requirements, various weights are always included at each price. Leading Foreign and American manufacturers have contributed to this extensive and complete range, covering every Hosiery demand of Men, Women and Children. An absolute match for any difficult shade of costume or slipper is guaranteed in Plain Silk Hose at $2.00 per pair; ten days being required to execute the order.

Women's "Betalph" Silk Hosiery

5201 "Betalph" White and all the Fashionable Colors in Silk, per pair $2.00
5202 "Betalph" Black Silk, per pair, $1.75; better quality, $2.50; extra size $2.25
5203 Black or White Silk Hose, with self or colored clocks, per pair, $1.75 and . . . $2.25

Women's Plain Silk Hosiery

5204 Black, White, Smoke, Bronze or Tan Silk, with deep lisle tops and soles, per pair . . . $ .50
5205 Black, White or Colors, with cotton soles and tops; very durable, per pair . . . . . . $ .95
5206 Black, White and all fashionable colors, double soles and tops, per pair $1.00
5207 Black, heavy and medium weight, double soles and tops, per pair $1.35
5208 Black, White or Colored, with cotton soles and tops, per pair $1.35

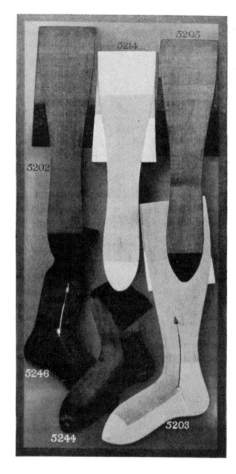

Women's Plain Silk Hosiery

5209 Black, White or Colored, double soles and tops, per pair $1.50
5210 Black, medium and light weight, double soles and tops, per pair $1.75
5211 Black or White, very fine; double soles and tops, per pair, $2.25 and upward.

Women's Plain Lisle Hosiery

5212 Black, White or Tan, double soles and tops, per pair, 25c. and 35c.; or 3 pairs for . . . $1.00
5213 Black, White, Tan, Bronze, Smoke, Pink or Sky-blue, double soles and tops, per pair . $ .50
5214 Black, White or Tan, double soles and tops, per pair, 75c. and $1.00
5215 Black, better qualities, double soles and tops, per pair, $1.25, $1.50 and upward.

Women's Plain Cotton Hosiery

5216 Black, White, Tan or Unbleached, double soles and tops, per pair, 25c. and 35c.; or 3 pairs for $1.00
5217 Black, White, Tan or Unbleached, double soles and tops, per pair . . . . $ .50
5218 Black, White or Tan, double soles and tops, better quality, per pair . . . . $ .75
5219 Black, very fine, double soles and tops, per pair, $1.00, $1.15, $1.25 and upward.
5220 Women's Black Plain Cotton Hose, unbleached soles, pair, 25c., 35c. (or 3 pairs for $1.00) and . . . . $ .50

WOMEN'S EXTRA SIZE HOSIERY

5221 Black, White, Tan or Unbleached Cotton, double soles and tops, per pair, 35c.; or 3 pairs for . $1.00
5222 Black, White or Tan Cotton, double soles and tops, per pair, 50c. and 75
5223 Black Cotton, with unbleached soles, pair, 50c. .75
5224 Black, White or Tan Cotton, trunk tops, per pair .50
5225 Black Cotton, double soles and tops, per pair, $1.00 and upward.
5226 Black, White or Tan Lisle, double soles and tops, 35c. (3 pairs for $1.00) and 50c. 75

5227 Black Lisle, better qualities, double soles and tops, per pair, $1.00 and upward.
5228 Black, White and Prevailing Colors in Silk, with cotton soles and tops, 95c.; better quality, black only $1.75
5229 Black, White, Tan or Colored Silk, double soles and tops, per pair, $1.35, $2.00 and 3.00
5230 Black or White Silk, double soles and tops, trunk tops, per pair, $1.75; heavy weight, black only 2.00

MEN'S COTTON, LISLE, WOOL AND SILK HALF-HOSE

Lisle and Plain Cotton Half-hose

5231 Black Cotton, Unbleached, White or Tan, double soles, 25c., 35c. (3 pairs for $1.00) and $ .50
5232 Black Cotton, better qualities, per pair, 60c. and .75
5233 Black Cotton, very fine, per pair, 95c., $1.15 and upward.
5234 Black Cotton, with unbleached soles, per pair, 25c., 35c. (3 pairs for $1.00) and 50
5235 Black Lisle, per pair 25
5236 Black, White or Colored Lisle, per pair, 35c. (3 pairs for $1.00) and 50
5237 Black Lisle, better qualities, per pair, 75c., 85c. 1.15
5238 Fancy French Lisle, in a variety of styles, pair 1.50

Summer Weight Cashmere and Silk

5239 Black Cashmere, light weight, per pair, 50c. and $ .60
5240 Black or Clerical Silk and Wool Mixed, per pair 1.50
5241 Natural Wool, light weight, per pair 60
5242 White Wool Tennis Socks, per pair, $1.00 and 1.25
5243 Black or Colored Silk, cotton soles and tops, per pair 50
5244 Black or Colored Silk, cotton soles, per pair . 1.00
5245 Black Silk, per pair, $1.35 and 1.65
5246 Black, White or Colored Silk, with hand-embroidered clocks, per pair, $1.75 and . . . 2.50
5247 Two-toned Silk, in a large variety of color combinations, per pair 2.00
5248 "Betalph" Black or Colored Silk Half-hose, pair 1.75

Men's Wool Golf Hose, in a large variety of styles, per pair $1.75 and upward

INFANTS' AND CHILDREN'S SOCKS AND STOCKINGS

No.	Descriptions	4	4½	5	5½	6	6½	7	7½	8	8½	9	9½	10	10½
5249	Black, White or Tan Ribbed Cotton Hose, double knees (black or tan from size 5½ up), per pair			$ .25	.25	.25	.25	.25	.25	.25	.25	.25	.25	.25	$ .25
5250	Black Cotton Hose, broad or narrow ribbed, double knees, per pair						.35	.35	.35	.35	.35	.35	.35	.40	.45
5251	Black, White or Tan Ribbed Cotton Hose, light weight, double knees, per pair						.30	.32	.34	.36	.38	.40	.42	.45	
5252	Black English Derby Ribbed Cotton Hose, per pair						.52	.55	.57	.60	.65	.70	.75	.80	.85
5253	White or Tan English Derby Ribbed Cotton Hose, per pair						.65	.70	.75	.80	.85	.90	.95	1.00	
5254	Black, White or Tan Plain Cotton Hose (black or tan from size 6½ up), per pair	$ .22	.24	.26	.28	.30	.32	.34	.36	.38	.40	.45	.50		
5255	Black, White or Tan Ribbed Lisle Hose (black or tan from size 6 up), per pair		.35	.35	.35	.35	.35	.35	.35	.35	.35	.35	.35	.35	
5256	Black, White or Tan Ribbed or Plain Lisle Hose (black or tan from size 6 up), per pair			.50	.50	.50	.50	.50	.50	.50	.50	.50	.50		
5257	White or Tan Cashmere Hose, ribbed summer weight, per pair		.25	.25	.25	.25	.25								
5258	White, Tan, Pink or Sky-blue Ribbed Silk and Wool Hose, summer weight, per pair		.35	.35	.35	.35	.35								
5259	White Merino Hose, English make, summer weight (also other grades), per pair	.45	.47	.50	.52	.55	.57	.60	.65	.70	.75				
5260	Black, White, Pink or Sky-blue Silk Hose, medium weight, per pair					1.35	1.35	1.35	1.35	1.35	1.35	1.35	1.35		
5261	Black, White, Pink or Sky-blue Socks (black from size 6½ up), per pair	1.00	1.00	1.00	1.00	1.25	1.25	1.25	1.50	1.50	1.50	1.50			
5262	White, Pink or Sky-blue Spun Silk Socks, per pair	.50	.50	.50	.50	.50	.50	.50	.50	.50	.50				

5263 to 5263E Children's Fancy Cotton or Lisle Socks, per pair, 25c., 35c. and 50c.

Black, White or Tan Cotton Socks, per pair, 25c., 35c. and upwards.   Black, White or Tan Lisle Socks, per pair, 25c., 35c. and upwards

MEN'S AND BOYS' UNDERGARMENTS
Sizes: Shirts, 34 to 46; Drawers, 30 to 46

5301	White Cotton Gauze Shirts, short sleeves or sleeveless	$ .45
5302	White Cotton Gauze Drawers, knee or ankle length	.45
5303	White Cotton Gauze Shirts, short sleeves or sleeveless	.75
5304	White Cotton Gauze Drawers, to match shirts No. 5303	1.00
5305	White Lisle Thread Shirts, short sleeves or sleeveless	1.00
5306	White Lisle Thread Drawers, to match shirts No. 5305	1.00
5307	White Lisle Thread Shirts, short sleeves or sleeveless	1.35
5308	White Lisle Thread Drawers, to match shirts No. 5307	1.35
5309	Balbriggan Shirts and Drawers, light weight; shirt with long or short sleeves, each	.50
5310	Balbriggan Shirts and Drawers, light weight; shirt with long or short sleeves, each	1.00
5311	Gray Merino Shirts and Drawers, light weight; shirts with long or short sleeves, each	$ .85
5312	White Merino Shirts, light weight, long or short sleeves	1.25
5313	White Merino Drawers, same quality as shirts No. 5312	1.35
5314	Plaid Madras Shirts, sleeveless, coat style, 50c. and	.75
5315	Plaid Madras Drawers, knee length, 50c. and	.75
5316	Jean Muslin Drawers, ankle length, with elastic anklets	.50
5317	Nainsook Union Suits, sleeveless and knee length, $1.00 and	1.25
5318	White Cotton Ribbed Union Suits, half sleeves, knee or three-quarter length; sleeveless, knee length, $1.00, $1.50 and	2.00

BOYS' UNDERGARMENTS
Open Front Drawers, for Boys 10 to 16 years of age

5319	White Cotton Gauze Shirts, with short sleeves or sleeveless	$ .35
5320	White Cotton Gauze Drawers, knee length only	.35
5321	White Cotton Gauze Shirts, sleeveless	.65
5322	White Cotton Gauze Drawers, knee length	.75
5323	Nainsook Shirts and Drawers, shirts sleeveless, coat style, drawers knee length, each	.40
5324	Nainsook Union Suits, sleeveless and knee length	.75
5325	White Cotton Ribbed Union Suits, sleeveless and knee length, 50c. and	1.00

BOYS' CLOTHING DEPARTMENT

5401 Tan Linen Coat Suit, with collar, and separate vestee of fancy white piqué; sizes, 4 to 8 years $3.75

5402 Junior Norfolk Tub Suit, of khaki, tan or gun-metal linen; sizes, 6 to 10 years $4.25

5402A Same model as above, in blue linen or white rep; sizes, 6 to 10 years $5.50

5403 Junior Norfolk Russian Suit, of blue chambray, with soft white rep collar, box plaits back and pocketed front; sizes, 4 to 8 years 3.50

5404 Boy's Single Breasted Raincoat, of tan rubberized cloth, with side pockets; sizes, 4 to 18 years 4.75

5404A Sou'wester Hat, to match raincoat No. 5404; sizes, 6½ to 7⅛ . . .75

5404B Boy's Separate Middy Blouse, of white or blue galatea; sizes, 4 to 10 years (not illustrated) 1.25

5405 Boy's Norfolk Tub Suit, of white duck, tan crash linen, light or dark khaki; sizes, 7 to 16 years 3.25

5405A Similar model, in tan or gun-metal linen; sizes, 7 to 16 years 4.25

5406 Boy's Norfolk Suit, all-wool, gray or brown fancy mixtures, with mohair lining and one extra pair of knickerbocker trousers; sizes. 7 to 16 years; at the special price of . . $6.50

5406A Norfolk Suit, similar to above, in gray tweed or brown homespun, with two pairs of knickerbockers; sizes, 7 to 16 years . . 7.50

5406B Norfolk Suit, same model as illustration No. 5406; of black and white worsted check, with two pairs of knickerbockers; sizes, 8 to 16 years 10.00

5407 Boy's Riding Suit, of khaki, attractive model, with breeches thoroughly reinforced 8.50

5408 Boy's Suit, including extra pair of knickerbockers; of stylish brown mixture or checked over plaid, with belt and patch pockets; sizes, 7 to 16 years 8.50

5408A Model similar to illustration No. 5408, of navy blue serge, with one pair of knickerbockers; sizes, 7 to 16 years 7.50

5408B Same as No. 5408A, with two pairs of knickerbockers 8.50

5409 Boy's Blue Serge Naval Reefer, with washable sailor collar conveniently detachable, sleeve emblem and brass buttons; sizes, 3 to 8 years; special, at . . . 5.50

5409A Similar model to above, with plain notch coat collar; in smart gray and tan woolen mixtures, also popular black and white checks; sizes, 3 to 8 years 6.75

This department maintains a large and comprehensive assortment of Boys' Woolen Suits in a wide range of materials for Spring and Summer at prices ranging from $6.50 to $18.50
A special feature is made of Blue Serge Suits, ranging in price from $7.50 to $16.50

5420   Middy Suit, with long sailor pants, of white galatea, with blue galatea collar and cuffs, black silk tie; sizes, 3 to 8 years . $3.75

5420A Similar model, of same material, with collar, cuffs and short straight pants of blue galatea; sizes, 3 to 8 years $2.75

5420B Similar model, in all white galatea, with black silk tie 2.75

5420C Middy Suit, similar model, blouse of neat woven stripe gingham, in blue and white or brown and white, with collar, cuffs and short pants of plain color chambray to match, black silk tie; sizes, 4 to 8 years $2.25

5420D Same model, in oyster white, tan linen or very fine blue linen finished chambray; sizes, 4 to 8 years 3.75

5421   New Style Short Russian Blouse Suit, of blue chambray, with white collar, and lowered belt; very smart; sizes, 2½ to 5 years 2.25

5421A Similar model, more elaborately trimmed, of excellent quality brown mixed chambray; sizes, 2½ to 6 years 3.50

5422   White Linene Beach Sailor Suit, trimmed with blue; sizes, 6 to 9 years 1.90

5422A Same model, middy style, with long sleeves and untrimmed pants; sizes, 3 to 7 years 1.90

5423   Blue Linen Suit, with white rep collar and cuffs, effective black silk tie and large white pearl buttons; sizes, 3 to 7 years   5 00

5423A Same style as above, in brown linen 5.00

5423B Similar style to No. 5423, in tan linen 3.75

BOYS' CLOTHING DEPARTMENT — (Continued)

5424   Tan Linen Middy Suit, with navy blue collar and cuffs; sizes, 4 to 7 years . . . $3.50

5425   White Rep Suit, in snappy coat style, with attached collar and vestee of blue chambray; sizes, 3 to 7 years; special price 2.25

5426   Dutch Suit, with white rep blouse; pants, collar and cuffs of blue chambray; sizes, 3 to 6 years 1.65

5426A Same style, of all white rep. 1.65

5427   Boy's Light Weight Naval Coat, of excellent quality dark blue cheviot, inverted plait belted in at center back; yoke and sleeves silk lined; an unusually attractive model; sizes, 4 to 10 years   10.50

5427A Blue Cheviot Hat, as illustrated; sizes, 6⅜ to 7 . . . . .   2.00

5428   Blue and White Woven Stripe Gingham Suit, with cadet blue collar and cuffs; sizes, 4 to 7 years 1.90

5429   Middy Suit, of blue chambray, with white rep collar and cuffs, yoke front, fastened with pearl links; sizes, 3 to 8 years . .   2.00

5429A Same model, in blue or tan linen 3.75

Not Illustrated

5430   Boy's Overalls, in tan or blue denim; sizes, 4 to 12 years . . $ .60

5431   Boy's Straight Pants, of khaki, white duck, tan linen or tan crash; sizes, 5 to 8 years 75

5431A Knickerbockers, same materials as above; sizes, 8 to 15 years   .95

BOYS' HATS AND FURNISHINGS

5450	Boy's Rah Rah Hat, of blue or white straw, with colored band; sizes, 6¼ to 7 . .	$1.50
5450A	Boy's Rah Rah Hat, in white duck, tan linen, gray crash and khaki, with colored band	.50
5451	Boy's High Crown Middy Hat, exceptionally good style, in white, with blue band;	
	blue, brown or black straw; sizes, 6⅜ to 7	3.50
5452	Boy's White Straw Hat, with neat black band; sizes, 6⅝ to 7⅛	1.75
5453	Boy's Hat, of blue straw, or white straw with blue band; sizes, 6¼ to 7; special	1.25
5454	Boy's Felt Hat, blue, green or brown; may be worn in telescope or Alpine shape; sizes, 6⅝ to 7⅛	2.00
5455	Boy's Stitched Cloth Hat, in brown or gray tweed mixture; sizes, 6½ to 7⅛	1.50
5501	Madras Blouses, in white ground with colored stripings; attached collar, 50c. and .	.95
5502	Madras Blouses, in plain white or colored stripes, with separate collars; sizes, 7 to 14 years; 95c. and	.75
5503	Flannel Outing Shirts, in gray or brown, with attached collar	1.50
5504	Sports Shirts, in plain white cheviot or soisette; 12 to 14 collar	1.35
5505	Negligee Shirts, in plain white mercerized materials; attached collar and soft turnback cuffs .	.95
5506	Fancy Negligee Shirts, of madras; detachable soft collar	.95
5507	Pajamas, in silk trimmed plain mercerized materials; tan or blue; sizes, 4 to 16 years . . .	1.50
5508	Fancy Madras Pajamas; sizes, 4 to 16 years	.95
5509	Night Shirts, of cambric, trimmed; sizes, 4 to 16 years	.50
5510 and 5511	Soft Outing Collars, white; sizes, 12 to 13½, per dozen, $1.50; each	.15
5512	Eton Collars; sizes, 11½ to 13½; per dozen, $1.50; each	.15
5513 and 5514	Silk Windsor Ties, in fancy plaids, 25c. and 50c.; popular plain colors, 25c. and . . .	.45
5515	Open-end Four-in-hand Scarfs, in plain colors	.25
5515A	Open-end Silk Scarfs, in attractive designs, 50c. and	.38
5516	Washable Four-in-hand Ties, plain white or fancy effects	.25
5517	Sampson Supporters; sizes, 4 to 10 years, 50c.; 12 to 14 years	.65
5518	Leather Belts, in black or tan; sizes, 26, 28 and 30; 50c. and	.75
5519	Two-piece Worsted Bathing Suits, in navy blue, with red or white borders; sizes, 8 to 16 years	2.25
5519A	One-piece Suit, as above; sizes, 2 to 8 years	2.25
5520	Sweater Coats, gray, with shawl collar; sizes, 26 to 34, $3.00; with V-neck	2.50
5521	Turkish Toweling Bath Robes, pink or blue effects; sizes, 4 to 8 years, $2.00; 10 to 18 years .	2.50
5522	Turkish Toweling Bath Slippers	1.00
5523	Plain Negligee Shirts, of white madras, with attached cuffs (not illustrated)	.95
5524	Plain Negligee Shirts, of fancy madras, with attached cuffs (not illustrated)	1.35
5525	Fancy Mercerized Negligee Shirts, with or without attached collar (not illustrated)	1.50
5526	Suspenders, plain white or fancy; 6, 8 and 10 years, 25c.; 12, 14 and 16 years (not illustrated) .	.45
5527	Madras Blouses, in plain white, with attached collar (not illustrated)	.75
5528	Plaited Blouses, in plain white madras, with stiff cuffs (not illustrated); $1.25 and . . .	.75
5529	Boy's Golf Cap, brown or gray tweed mixtures; blue serge; 6⅜ to 7⅛ (not illustrated); 65c., $1.00	1.50

Boys' Shirts, with neckbands, 12 to 14 inches. Shirts, with collars attached, 12½ to 14 inches. Blouses, 7 to 14 years

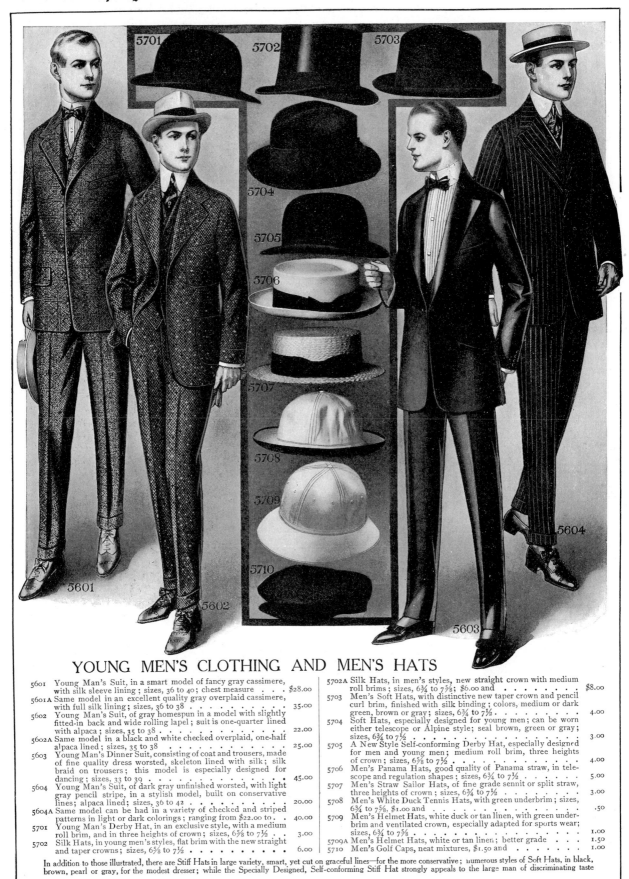

YOUNG MEN'S CLOTHING AND MEN'S HATS

5601 Young Man's Suit, in a smart model of fancy gray cassimere, with silk sleeve lining; sizes, 36 to 40; chest measure . . . $28.00

5601A Same model in an excellent quality gray overplaid cassimere, with full silk lining; sizes, 36 to 38 . . . . 35.00

5602 Young Man's Suit, of gray homespun in a model with slightly fitted-in back and wide rolling lapel; suit is one-quarter lined with alpaca; sizes, 35 to 38 . . . . 22.00

5602A Same model in a black and white checked overplaid, one-half alpaca lined; sizes, 35 to 38 . . . . 25.00

5603 Young Man's Dinner Suit, consisting of coat and trousers, made of fine quality dress worsted, skeleton lined with silk; silk braid on trousers; this model is especially designed for dancing; sizes, 33 to 39 . . . . 45.00

5604 Young Man's Suit, of dark gray unfinished worsted, with light gray pencil stripe, in a stylish model, built on conservative lines; alpaca lined; sizes, 36 to 42 . . . . 20.00

5604A Same model can be had in a variety of checked and striped patterns in light or dark colorings; ranging from $22.00 to . . 40.00

5701 Young Man's Derby Hat, in an exclusive style, with a medium roll brim, and in three heights of crown; sizes, 6⅝ to 7½ . 3.00

5702 Silk Hats, in young men's styles, flat brim with the new straight and taper crowns; sizes, 6⅝ to 7½ 6.00

5702A Silk Hats, in men's styles, new straight crown with medium roll brims; sizes, 6¾ to 7⅝; $6.00 and $8.00

5703 Men's Soft Hats, with distinctive new taper crown and pencil curl brim, finished with silk binding; colors, medium or dark green, brown or gray; sizes, 6¾ to 7½ 4.00

5704 Soft Hats, especially designed for young men; can be worn either telescope or Alpine style; seal brown, green or gray; sizes, 6¾ to 7½ 3.00

5705 A New Style Self-conforming Derby Hat, especially designed for men and young men; medium roll brim, three heights of crown; sizes, 6⅝ to 7½ 4.00

5706 Men's Panama Hats, good quality of Panama straw, in telescope and regulation shapes; sizes, 6¾ to 7½ 5.00

5707 Men's Straw Sailor Hats, of fine grade sennit or split straw, three heights of crown; sizes, 6¾ to 7½ 3.00

5708 Men's White Duck Tennis Hats, with green underbrim; sizes, 6¾ to 7⅝, $1.00 and 50

5709 Men's Helmet Hats, white duck or tan linen, with green underbrim and ventilated crown, especially adapted for sports wear; sizes, 6¾ to 7⅝ 1.00

5709A Men's Helmet Hats, white or tan linen; better grade . . . 1.50

5710 Men's Golf Caps, neat mixtures, $1.50 and 1.00

In addition to those illustrated, there are Stiff Hats in large variety, smart, yet cut on graceful lines—for the more conservative; numerous styles of Soft Hats, in black, brown, pearl or gray, for the modest dresser; while the Specially Designed, Self-conforming Stiff Hat strongly appeals to the large man of discriminating taste

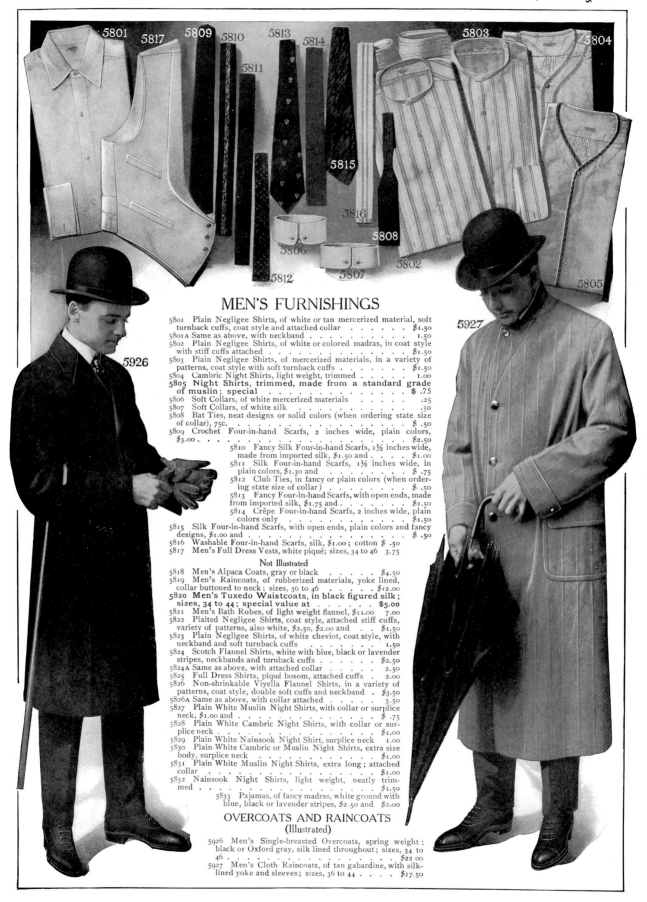

MEN'S FURNISHINGS

5801 Plain Negligee Shirts, of white or tan mercerized material, soft
      turnback cuffs, coat style and attached collar $1.50
5801A Same as above, with neckband 1.50
5802 Plain Negligee Shirts, of white or colored madras, in coat style
      with stiff cuffs attached $1.50
5803 Plain Negligee Shirts, of mercerized materials, in a variety of
      patterns, coat style with soft turnback cuffs $1.50
5804 Cambric Night Shirts, light weight, trimmed 1.00
5805 **Night Shirts, trimmed, made from a standard grade
      of muslin; special** . . . . $ .75
5806 Soft Collars, of white mercerized materials 25
5807 Soft Collars, of white silk 50
5808 Bat Ties, neat designs or solid colors (when ordering state size
      of collar), 75c. $ .50
5809 Crochet Four-in-hand Scarfs, 2 inches wide, plain colors,
      $3.00 . . . . $2.50
5810 Fancy Silk Four-in-hand Scarfs, 1½ inches wide,
      made from imported silk, $1.50 and $1.00
5811 Silk Four-in-hand Scarfs, 1½ inches wide, in
      plain colors, $1.30 and . . . . $ .75
5812 Club Ties, in fancy or plain colors (when order-
      ing state size of collar) . . . . $ .50
5813 Fancy Four-in-hand Scarfs, with open ends, made
      from imported silk, $1.75 and $1.50
5814 Crêpe Four-in-hand Scarfs, 2 inches wide, plain
      colors only $1.50
5815 Silk Four-in-hand Scarfs, with open ends, plain colors and fancy
      designs, $1.00 and . . . . $ .50
5816 Washable Four-in-hand Scarfs, silk, $1.00 ; cotton $ .50
5817 Men's Full Dress Vests, white piqué; sizes, 34 to 46 3.75

Not Illustrated

5818 Men's Alpaca Coats, gray or black $4.50
5819 Men's Raincoats, of rubberized materials, yoke lined,
      collar buttoned to neck ; sizes, 36 to 46 . . . $12.00
5820 **Men's Tuxedo Waistcoats, in black figured silk;
      sizes, 34 to 44; special value at** $5.00
5821 Men's Bath Robes, of light weight flannel, $11.00 7.00
5822 Plaited Negligee Shirts, coat style, attached stiff cuffs,
      variety of patterns, also white, $2.50, $2.00 and . . $1.50
5823 Plain Negligee Shirts, of white cheviot, coat style, with
      neckband and soft turnback cuffs 1.50
5824 Scotch Flannel Shirts, white with blue, black or lavender
      stripes, neckbands and turnback cuffs $2.50
5824A Same as above, with attached collar 2.50
5825 Full Dress Shirts, piqué bosom, attached cuffs . 2.00
5826 Non-shrinkable Viyella Flannel Shirts, in a variety of
      patterns, coat style, double soft cuffs and neckband . $3.50
5826A Same as above, with collar attached 3.50
5827 Plain White Muslin Night Shirts, with collar or surplice
      neck, $1.00 and . . . . $ .75
5828 Plain White Cambric Night Shirts, with collar or sur-
      plice neck $1.00
5829 Plain White Nainsook Night Shirt, surplice neck 1.00
5830 Plain White Cambric or Muslin Night Shirts, extra size
      body, surplice neck $1.00
5831 Plain White Muslin Night Shirts, extra long ; attached
      collar $1.00
5832 Nainsook Night Shirts, light weight, neatly trim-
      med $1.50
5833 Pajamas, of fancy madras, white ground with
      blue, black or lavender stripes, $2.50 and $2.00

OVERCOATS AND RAINCOATS
(Illustrated)

5926 Men's Single-breasted Overcoats, spring weight ;
      black or Oxford gray, silk lined throughout; sizes, 34 to
      46 . . . . $22.00
5927 Men's Cloth Raincoats, of tan gabardine, with silk-
      lined yoke and sleeves; sizes, 36 to 44 . . . . $17.50

MEN'S FURNISHINGS
(Continued)

5851 Pajamas, of fancy madras, white ground with blue, black or lavender stripes, also plain white . . . $1.50

5852 Pajamas, in fine quality of blue, white, tan or lavender mercerized materials $1.50

5901 Men's Heather-mixed Sweaters, Shetland wool, V-neck; special $6.00

5902 Men's Gray Worsted Coat Sweaters, with V-neck $4.50

5903 Men's Sweater-knit Swimming Suits, pure worsted, in gray or navy blue, with plain and fancy borders $5.75

5904 Men's Worsted Bathing Suits, in plain colors or striped borders $3.00

5905 Men's Imported Toweling Bath Robes, with neat fancy stripes $3.75

5905A Men's Imported Toweling Bath Robes, better quality, in fancy stripes $5.00

5906 Men's Toweling Bath Slippers, with corduroy pipings $1.00

5907 Men's Leather Belts, black or tan, $1.00 and 50

5908 Men's White Serge Outing Trousers, with neat stripes $5.00

5908A Men's White Flannel Outing Trousers ; special value $5.00

5909 Men's Riding Breeches, of moleskin cloth, in olive shades, reinforced seat and legs $4.50

5909A Men's Riding Breeches, in tan khaki, with heavily reinforced seat and legs, $3.50; heavier weight $4.50

5910 Wool Steamer Rug, in plaid design, with reverse side of plain blue, gray or brown ; very special $5.50

5911 Motor Robes, light weight, in Oxford gray or tan whipcord effects ; size, 84-inch, $8.00 ; 68-inch $6.50

Not Illustrated

5834 Plain Negligee Shirts, of fancy or white madras, coat style, detachable cuffs $1.50

5835 Pajamas, of plain white, tan or blue mercerized material, in slip-on style, V-neck, no buttons on coat $1.75

5836 Plain White Muslin or Nainsook Night Shirts, in slip-on style, V-neck, no buttons in front . . . $1.00

A large assortment of Men's Fancy Negligee Shirts, with soft cuffs, is carried in stock, comprising silk, silk-mixed and mercerized materials, at prices ranging from $1.50 to $9.00 each.

NOTE—Men's Shirts are carried in neck sizes 14 to 17½ inches, inclusive

5837 Open End Four-in-hand Scarfs, in black grosgrain or barathea, $1.75 . . . . $1.00

5838 Black Silk Four-in-hand Scarfs ; 1½, 1¾ and 2 inches wide ; 75c. 50

5839 Fancy Foulard Open End Four-in-hand Scarfs, in black and white or navy and white, neat designs or dots 1.50

5840 Fancy Crêpe Open End Four-in-hand Scarfs, in rich colorings 1.50

Aside from the staple and long accepted styles in Collars, which are always carried in large variety, there are all the newest shapes and variations for the man who keeps abreast with Fashion. Domestic makes, per dozen, $1.50 and $2.75. English makes, per dozen, $3.50.

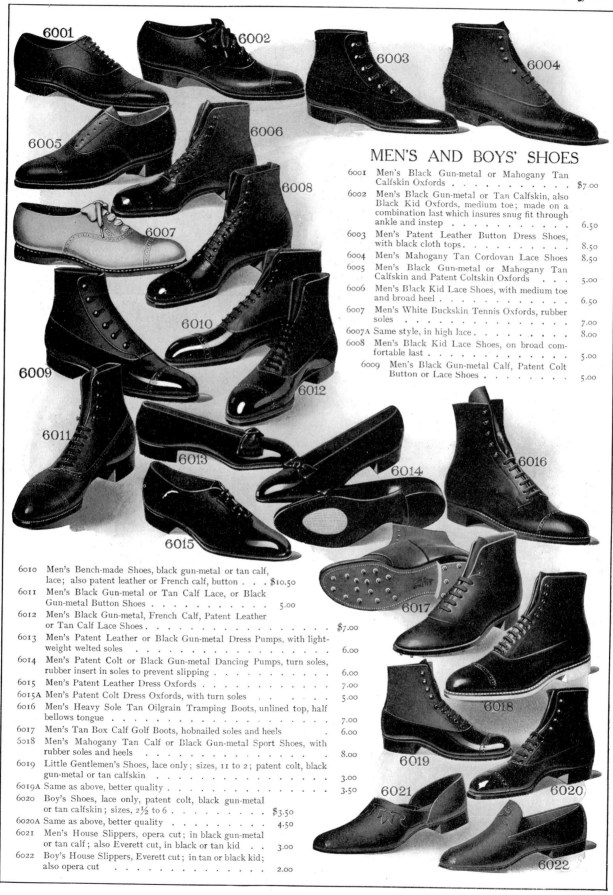

MEN'S AND BOYS' SHOES

6001   Men's Black Gun-metal or Mahogany Tan Calfskin Oxfords $7.00

6002   Men's Black Gun-metal or Tan Calfskin, also Black Kid Oxfords, medium toe; made on a combination last which insures snug fit through ankle and instep 6.50

6003   Men's Patent Leather Button Dress Shoes, with black cloth tops 8.50

6004   Men's Mahogany Tan Cordovan Lace Shoes   8.50

6005   Men's Black Gun-metal or Mahogany Tan Calfskin and Patent Coltskin Oxfords . . . 5.00

6006   Men's Black Kid Lace Shoes, with medium toe and broad heel 6.50

6007   Men's White Buckskin Tennis Oxfords, rubber soles 7.00

6007A   Same style, in high lace 8.00

6008   Men's Black Kid Lace Shoes, on broad comfortable last 5.00

6009   Men's Black Gun-metal Calf, Patent Colt Button or Lace Shoes 5.00

6010   Men's Bench-made Shoes, black gun-metal or tan calf, lace; also patent leather or French calf, button . . . $10.50

6011   Men's Black Gun-metal or Tan Calf Lace, or Black Gun-metal Button Shoes 5.00

6012   Men's Black Gun-metal, French Calf, Patent Leather or Tan Calf Lace Shoes $7.00

6013   Men's Patent Leather or Black Gun-metal Dress Pumps, with light-weight welted soles 6.00

6014   Men's Patent Colt or Black Gun-metal Dancing Pumps, turn soles, rubber insert in soles to prevent slipping 6.00

6015   Men's Patent Leather Dress Oxfords 7.00

6015A   Men's Patent Colt Dress Oxfords, with turn soles 5.00

6016   Men's Heavy Sole Tan Oilgrain Tramping Boots, unlined top, half bellows tongue 7.00

6017   Men's Tan Box Calf Golf Boots, hobnailed soles and heels   6.00

6018   Men's Mahogany Tan Calf or Black Gun-metal Sport Shoes, with rubber soles and heels 8.00

6019   Little Gentlemen's Shoes, lace only; sizes, 11 to 2; patent colt, black gun-metal or tan calfskin 3.00

6019A   Same as above, better quality 3.50

6020   Boy's Shoes, lace only, patent colt, black gun-metal or tan calfskin; sizes, 2½ to 6 . . . . $3.50

6020A   Same as above, better quality 4.50

6021   Men's House Slippers, opera cut; in black gun-metal or tan calf; also Everett cut, in black or tan kid . . 3.00

6022   Boy's House Slippers, Everett cut; in tan or black kid; also opera cut 2.00

SPORTING GOODS
GOLF, TENNIS AND POLO SUPPLIES

6101 Triple Insert Drivers and Brassies, giving attractiveness, efficiency and durability, non-hooking and non-slicing, additional distance and satisfaction in use, each $4.00
6102 Drivers, special weights and shafts, each 2.25
6103 Brassies, each 2.50
6104 Drivers and Brassies, made with an ivory face used by many leading players, gives the ball greater distance, similar to No. 6101, each $5.00
6105 to 6107 Irons, with selected shafts and specially prepared calf grips, each $2.00
6108 Special Putters, each 2.50
6109 Selected, Scotch and English clubs ; hand forged, each 2.25
6110 Liberty Golf Counters : Women's, Genuine Pigskin, each 1.50
6111 Liberty Golf Counters : Men's, Black Seal Grain or Genuine Pigskin, each $1.00
6112 Polo Sticks, good assortment, each 2.50
6113 Single Racket Presses, each 1.00
6114 and 6115 Show two styles of our Popular Rackets : The Gold Medal and Brooks. Other makes in stock are the All-Comers, Burke, Doherty, Davis Cup, Hackett and Alexander also Ward and Wright ; including waterproof cover, each $8.00
6116 Best Quality Russet Cowhide Bag, with ball pocket and sling to match ; removable hood for covering clubs ; fitted with patent buckle lock of heavy brass ; accepted by railroads as baggage $12.00
6117 Special Compartment Bag, with eleven entire length pockets for clubs, made from the best imported tan corduroy ; reinforced with strips of leather-covered steel ; brown leather trimmings ; brass fitted handle and shoulder strap ; hood specially designed to cover clubs securely ; ample ball pocket. Bag has umbrella attachment, and is sufficiently roomy for change of clothing $15.00
6118 Automatic Caddy Bag 5.00
6119 Juvenile Golf Sets, consisting of 3 clubs ; bag and 2 balls 5.00
6120 Parachute Ball, for practice 80
6121 Ball Cleaner, rubber pouch, sponge and brush 50
6122 Ball Cleaner, aluminum, with sponge 35
6123 Ball Cleaner, double rubber pouch, special inside felt to be saturated . . . . $ .50
6124 Captive Ball, for practice 1.00
6125 Simplex Ball Marker, impresses initials, but does not injure the ball ; price includes designated initials, each . . . $2.00
6126 Championship Tennis Balls, consisting of Spalding Championship, Wright & Ditson, Ayres, Slazenger and Taylor, each, 35c. ; 3 for $1.00 ; per dozen $4.00
6126A Practice Balls, each, 20c., 25c. and 30
6127 Rubber Handle Cover, for securing better grip 50

Not Illustrated

6128 Golf Balls, Colonel 31, Worthington Ace, or Whippet, each, 75c. ; per dozen $9.00
6129 Golf Balls, Arch Colonel, Black and Orange Ringer, Black Circle, or Midget Bramble, Glory, Baby Midget or Domino Dimples, each, 65c. ; per dozen $7.50
6130 Golf Balls, remade ; 3 for $1.00 ; per dozen 4.00
6131 Clock Golf, per set, $3.00, $5.00 and 10.00
6132 Tennis Nets, $3.50 to 12.00

A complete line of accessories pertaining to Golf, Tennis and Polo is maintained constantly in stock

THE KODAK AND ITS COMPLETE EQUIPMENT

Sporting Goods and Outing Supplies suggest the ever-companionable Kodak ; and the amateur photographer will find in conjunction with this department a complete line of Kodaks, films and supplies, including the Autochrom plates for reproducing natural colors

PERFUMES AND TOILET ARTICLES

Prices subject to change

For the Dressing Table, Bathroom or Nursery, no toilet article is more appreciated than that of French, English or American-made Celluloid. Complete sets are constantly maintained, or individual pieces may be selected — with a view to completing the set, if desired. The Celluloid offers a mellow background for initials or monograms, either of which will require two to three days; or pieces may be carved, as preferred

Brillantines

6201	Coty's L'Origan	$1.30
6202	Coty's La Rose Jacqueminot . . .	1.30
6203	Coty's Styx	1.30
6204	Houbigant's, 60c., 95c.	1.50
6205	Pinaud's, 30c.	.45
6206	Roger and Gallet's, 30c., 50c. . . .	.90

Rubber Goods

6207	Bath Sprays, 75c. to	$1.50
6208	Fountain Syringes, $1.35 to . . .	2.75
6209	Hot Water Bottles, 75c. to . . .	2.00
6210	Rubber Gloves, 75c.	1.00
6211	Air Cushions, assorted colors, $2.25 to	4.50
6212	Cretonne Tourist Cases, 85c. to . .	1.65
6213	Silk Tourist Cases, $1.75 to . . .	4.00
6214	Pullman Aprons, cretonne, 95c. to $2.00 ; satin, $1.75	3.25
6215	Cretonne Sponge Bags, 30c. to . .	.85
6216	Silk Sponge Bags, 55c. to . . .	1.25
6217	Cretonne Wash Cloth Cases, 25c. to	1.00
6218	Silk Wash Cloth Cases, 65c. to . .	1.50
6219	Bath Sponges, ranging in price from 25c. to	10.00
6220	A complete line of Hair Brushes, in assorted woods with French or English bristles, ranging in price from 50c. to	10.00
6221	Same as above in Clothes, also Hat Brushes, 50c. to	5.00
6222	Military Brushes, per pair, $1.50 to	15.00
6223	Bath Brushes, with or without handles, from 50c. to	5.00

Hair Tonics

6224	Hirsutus, 61c., $1.19	$2.31
6225	Mrs. Mason's Tonic	.74
6226	Miro Dena	1.00
6227	Ergen's Marshmallow, 66c.	1.50
6228	Pinaud's Eau de Quinine, 45c., 85c., $1.55	3.00
6229	Herbex	.45

Dentifrices

6230	Dr. Pierre's, 60c., $1.10, $1.75 . .	$3.60
6231	Fougera's Eau Angelique, 53c. . .	1.27
6232	Pinaud's, 40c., 70c.	1.20
6233	Coty's	1.40
6234	Colgate's, 25c.	.50

Toilet Powders

6235	Coty's La Rose Jacqueminot, in paper box, $1.55 and $3.10 ; in leather box	$4.65
6236	Coty's Jasmin de Corse, in paper box, $1.55 and $3.10 ; in leather box . .	4.65
6237	Coty's L'Effleurt, in paper box, $1.55 and $3.10 ; in leather box . .	4.65
6238	Coty's Styx, in paper box, $1.55 and $3.10 ; in leather box	4.65
6239	Coty's L'Or, in paper box, $1.55 and $3.10 ; in leather box	4.65
6240	Coty's, in various odors, in paper box	1.60
6241	Houbigant's Ideal	3.70
6242	Houbigant's Quelques Fleurs . . .	4.90
6243	Houbigant's Premier Mai	3.75
6244	Houbigant's La Rose France . . .	4.80
6245	Houbigant's Peau d'Espagne . . .	2.00
6246	Royal Houbigant	2.85
6247	Guerlain's Ladies in all Climates . .	1.90
6248	Guerlain's Cypris	1.35

Toilet Powders — (Continued)

6249	Violets Ambre Royal	$1.75
6250	Bourjois Manon Lescout	1.00
6251	Djer Kiss, 50c.	.85

Talcum Powders

6252	Houbigant's Cœur de Jeanette, La Rose France, Quelques Fleurs and Ideal	$ .75
6253	Guerlain's, Oeillet, Rose, and Violet	1.05

Liquid Powders

6254	Hudnut's Orchid Beauty Cream . .	$1.00
6255	Dorin's, 30c.	.60
6256	Miro Dena	1.00

Sachets

6257	Coty's La Rose Jacqueminot, bottle, $1.20	$3.05
6258	Coty's L'Origan, $1.20	3.05
6259	Coty's Styx, $1.40	3.05
6260	Coty's L'Or, $1.20	3.05
6261	Houbigant's Ideal, bottle	1.90
6262	Houbigant's La Rose France . . .	1.90
6263	Houbigant's Ideal, in satin envelope	3.85
6264	Houbigant's Quelques Fleurs . . .	1.90

Extracts

6265	Coty's La Rose Jacqueminot, bottle, $2.60, $5.00	$9.75
6266	Coty's Muguet, $2.60, $5.00 . . .	9.75
6267	Coty's L'Origan, $3.10, $5.00 . . .	9.75
6268	Coty's Violet Pourpre, $2.60, $5.00	9.75
6269	Coty's Jasmin de Corse	5.00
6270	Coty's L'Effleurt, $4.40	8.35
6271	Coty's Lilas Pourpre, $5.00 . . .	9.75
6272	Coty's Styx	12.85
6273	Coty's Ambre Antique, $12.85 . . .	25.75
6274	Coty's Le Nouveau Cyclamen . . .	7.50
6275	Coty's Oeillet	7.20
6276	L'Or, $3.10	5.30
6277	Coty's Assorted Odors, Peau d'Espagne, Chypre, Violette, Heliotrope, Lilac Blanc	3.10
6278	Houbigant's Ideal, $2.85, $4.90, $9.00	14.35
6279	Houbigant's Cœur de Jeanette, $2.10	3.60
6280	Houbigant's Premier Mai	4.90
6281	Houbigant's Royal Cyclamen . . .	4.90
6282	Houbigant's Violet Houbigant . .	7.00
6283	Houbigant's Quintessence de Violettes	6.15
6284	Houbigant's Quelques Fleurs, $3.75	6.95
6285	Houbigant's La Rose France . . .	7.45
6286	Houbigant's Evette	2.25
6287	Houbigant's Inconnu	7.75
6288	Houbigant's Muguet Parfum, non-alcoholic	1.90
6289	Houbigant's Rose Parfum, non-alcoholic	1.90
6290	Houbigant's Lilac Parfum, non-alcoholic	1.90
6291	Houbigant's Violet Parfum, non-alcoholic	2.35
6292	Guerlain's Quand-Vient L'été . . .	8.75
6293	Guerlain's Une Rose	8.75
6294	Guerlain's Rue de la Paix	8.75
6295	Guerlain's Fol Arome	10.25
6296	Guerlain's L'Heure Bleue	10.25
6297	Guerlain's Champs-Elysees . . .	12.50

Extracts — (Continued)

6298	Guerlain's Aprés L'Ondee	$5.50
6299	Guerlain's Jardin de Mon Curé . .	2.90
6300	Guerlain's Jicky, $1.95	2.95
6301	Guerlain's Mi Mai	7.25

Toilet Waters

6302	Coty's La Rose Jacqueminot, $2.60, $5.00	$10.00
6303	Coty's Styx, $5.00	10.00
6304	Coty's Muguet, $2.60, $5.00 . . .	10.00
6305	Coty's L'Origan, $2.60, $5.00 . . .	10.00
6306	Coty's Violette Pourpre, $2.60, $5.00	10.00
6307	Coty's Jasmin de Corse	5.00
6308	Coty's L'Effleurt, $2.60, $5.00 . . .	10.00
6309	Coty's Lilas Pourpre	5.00
6310	Coty's Ambre Antique	5.00
6311	Coty's Oeillet	5.00
6312	Houbigant's Ideal	4.65
6313	Houbigant's Cœur de Jeanette . .	4.65
6314	Houbigant's Premier Mai	5.00
6315	Houbigant's Quelques Fleurs . . .	6.15
6316	Houbigant's Violet Houbigant . .	6.70
6317	Houbigant's La Rose France . . .	6.00
6318	Houbigant's Peau d'Espagne . . .	1.75
6319	Houbigant's Violet Eau de Toilette .	1.80
6320	Guerlain's Aprés L'Ondee	2.25
6321	Guerlain's Jasmin	2.25
6322	Guerlain's Oeillet	2.25
6323	Guerlain's Gardenia	2.25
6324	Guerlain's Chypre	1.60

Colognes

6325	Houbigant's Eau de Cologne . . .	$1.50
6326	Houbigant's Ideal	3.30
6327	No. 4711 Eau de Cologne, 60c. . .	1.20
6328	Guerlain's Cologne, $1.25, $2.30 . .	3.40
6329	Guerlain's Verveine, $1.10	2.25
6330	Johanne Maria Farina Cologne, 37c., 75c.	1.50
6331	Madonna Farina Cologne, 37c., 75c.	1.50

Creams

6332	Créme Rhea, 45c., 90c.	$1.55
6333	Luxuria	.50
6334	Créme Simon, 35c., 72c.	.98
6335	Guerlain's Secret de Bonne Femme	1 65
6336	Miro Dena Skin Food, 50c. . . .	1.00
6337	Miro Dena Cold Cream	.50
6338	Hudnut's Marvelous Cream, 50c. . .	1.00

Toilet Soaps

6339	Houbigant's Ideal, cake	$2.75
6340	Houbigant's Cœur de Jeanette . .	2.25
6341	Houbigant's La Rose France . . .	3.25
6342	Houbigant's Quelques Fleurs . .	2.50
6343	Houbigant's Fougere Royal . . .	.50
6344	Roger & Gallet's Assorted Odors, cake	.25
6345	Roger & Gallet's Violette de Parme	.45
6346	Roger & Gallet's Vera Violetta and Assorted Odors	.85
6347	Coty's La Rose Jacqueminot . . .	1.80
6348	Coty's L'Origan	1.00
6349	Coty's Lilac Blanc, Heliotrope, Peau d'Espagne, Chypre and Violette	.50

Thermos Bottles

6350	Thermos Bottles, pint, $1.50 ; quart	$2.50
6351	Thermos Carafes	4.50

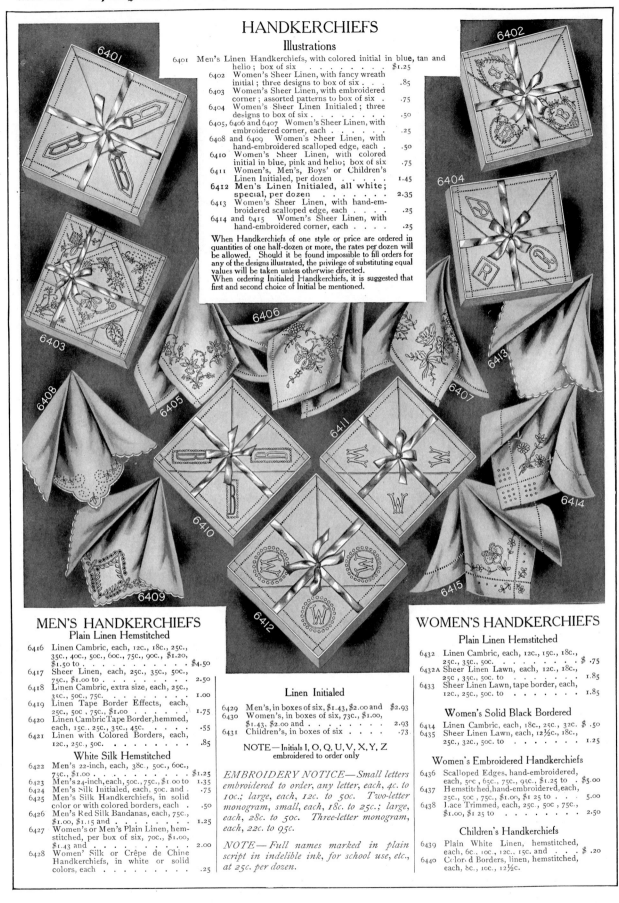

HANDKERCHIEFS
Illustrations

6401	Men's Linen Handkerchiefs, with colored initial in blue, tan and helio; box of six	$1.25
6402	Women's Sheer Linen, with fancy wreath initial; three designs to box of six	.85
6403	Women's Sheer Linen, with embroidered corner; assorted patterns to box of six	.75
6404	Women's Sheer Linen Initialed; three designs to box of six	.50
6405, 6406 and 6407	Women's Sheer Linen, with embroidered corner, each	.25
6408 and 6409	Women's Sheer Linen, with hand-embroidered scalloped edge, each	.50
6410	Women's Sheer Linen, with colored initial in blue, pink and helio; box of six	.75
6411	Women's, Men's, Boys' or Children's Linen Initialed, per dozen	1.45
6412	**Men's Linen Initialed, all white; special, per dozen**	2.35
6413	Women's Sheer Linen, with hand-embroidered scalloped edge, each	.25
6414 and 6415	Women's Sheer Linen, with hand-embroidered corner, each	.25

When Handkerchiefs of one style or price are ordered in quantities of one half-dozen or more, the rates per dozen will be allowed. Should it be found impossible to fill orders for any of the designs illustrated, the privilege of substituting equal values will be taken unless otherwise directed.

When ordering Initialed Handkerchiefs, it is suggested that first and second choice of Initial be mentioned.

MEN'S HANDKERCHIEFS
Plain Linen Hemstitched

6416	Linen Cambric, each, 12c., 18c., 25c., 35c., 40c., 50c., 60c., 75c., 90c., $1.20, $1.50 to	$4.50
6417	Sheer Linen, each, 25c., 35c., 50c., 75c., $1.00 to	2.50
6418	Linen Cambric, extra size, each, 25c., 35c., 50c., 75c.	1.00
6419	Linen Tape Border Effects, each, 25c., 50c., 75c., $1.00	1.75
6420	Linen Cambric Tape Border, hemmed, each, 15c., 25c., 35c., 45c.	.55
6421	Linen with Colored Borders, each, 12c., 25c., 50c.	.85

White Silk Hemstitched

6422	Men's 22-inch, each, 38c., 50c., 60c., 75c., $1.00	$1.25
6423	Men's 24-inch, each, 50c., 75c., $1.00 to	1.35
6424	Men's Silk Initialed, each, 50c. and	.75
6425	Men's Silk Handkerchiefs, in solid color or with colored borders, each	.50
6426	Men's Red Silk Bandanas, each, 75c., $1.00, $1.15 and	1.25
6427	Women's or Men's Plain Linen, hemstitched, per box of six, 70c., $1.00, $1.43 and	2.00
6428	Women' Silk or Crêpe de Chine Handkerchiefs, in white or solid colors, each	.25

Linen Initialed

6429	Men's, in boxes of six, $1.43, $2.00 and	$2.93
6430	Women's, in boxes of six, 73c., $1.00, $1.43, $2.00 and	2.93
6431	Children's, in boxes of six	.73

NOTE—Initials I, O, Q, U, V, X, Y, Z embroidered to order only

EMBROIDERY NOTICE—Small letters embroidered to order, any letter, each, 4c. to 10c.; large, each, 12c. to 50c. Two-letter monogram, small, each, 18c. to 25c.; large, each, 28c. to 50c. Three-letter monogram, each, 22c. to 95c.

NOTE—Full names marked in plain script in indelible ink, for school use, etc., at 25c. per dozen.

WOMEN'S HANDKERCHIEFS
Plain Linen Hemstitched

6432	Linen Cambric, each, 12c., 15c., 18c., 25c., 35c., 50c.	$ .75
6432A	Sheer Linen Lawn, each, 12c., 18c., 25c., 35c., 50c. to	1.85
6433	Sheer Linen Lawn, tape border, each, 12c., 25c., 50c. to	1.85

Women's Solid Black Bordered

6434	Linen Cambric, each, 18c., 25c., 32c.	$ .50
6435	Sheer Linen Lawn, each, 12½c., 18c., 25c., 32c., 50c. to	1.25

Women's Embroidered Handkerchiefs

6436	Scalloped Edges, hand-embroidered, each, 50c., 65c., 75c., 95c., $1.25 to	$5.00
6437	Hemstitched, hand-embroidered, each, 25c., 50c., 75c., $1.00, $1 25 to	5.00
6438	Lace Trimmed, each, 25c., 50c. 75c., $1.00, $1 25 to	2.50

Children's Handkerchiefs

6439	Plain White Linen, hemstitched, each, 6c., 10c., 12c., 15c. and	$ .20
6440	Colored Borders, linen, hemstitched, each, 8c., 10c., 12½c.	

SMALL WARES

The following enumerated articles represent only a limited portion of a completely equipped department, which is also prepared to furnish all similar merchandise in popular demand

Bathing Caps and Slippers

6501	Rubber Caps; plain, each, 45c.; skull shape	$ .35
6502	Silk; plain, each, 50c.; handkerchiefs, 90c. and	1.35
6503	Satin, turban shape, to tie: each	2.00
6504	Bathing Hat, of satin, with wire brim; each	1.25
6505	Bathing Slippers, canvas, black or white; pair	.50
6506	Bathing Slippers, black satin; pair, $1.45 and	2.25

Sewing Silk, Heminway's

		EACH	DOZ.
6507	Sewing Silk, 100-yard spools	$ .09	$ .95
6508	Buttonhole Twist, 20-yard spools	.05	.50
6509	Sewing Silk, 1-ounce spools	.58	6.40
6510	Sewing Silk, ½-ounce spools	.30	3.20
6511	Darning Silk, on spools	.05	.55
6512	Darning Silk, black, white, or tan; in boxes		.35

Sewing and Darning Cottons

		EACH	DOZ.
6513	Clark's "O. N. T.," 200-yard spools	$ .05	$ .55
6514	Brook's Glacé, 200-yard spools	.05	.55
6515	Basting Cotton, 500-yard spools	.05	.55
6516	Kerr's Luster-twist, 300-yard spools	.10	1.15
6517	Wound Bobbins, box	.05	.58
6518	Darning Cotton, mercerized; in boxes, black, white or tan, 20c. per box; in balls, all colors	.10	1.10
6519	Darning Cotton, in balls	.02	.22
6520	Spool Cotton, six in case		.55

Needles, Tapes and Hooks and Eyes

6521	Needles, Milward's or Roberts'; paper, 4c.; dozen	$ .45
6522	Needle Cases, Milward's; each, 35c., 50c.	1.00
6523	Tape, cotton, 4-yard pieces, ¼ to 1¼-inch; each, 3c. to	.09
6524	Tape, cotton, 10-yard pieces, ¼ to 1 inch; each, 6c. to	.12
6525	Tape, linen, 3-yard pieces, ⅛ to 1¼-inch; each, 3c. to	.13
6526	Linen Bobbin, 2-yard pieces; dozen, 10c. and	.15
6527	Bias Lawn Tape, 12-yard pieces, ¼ to ½ inch; each, 15c. to	.30
6528	Hooks and Eyes, Niagara; card, each	.10
6529	Hooks and Eyes, on tape; yard	.25
6530	Ball and Socket Fasteners; dozen, 4c.; extra quality	.10

Braids, Bindings, Beltings and Elastics

6531	White or Colored Silk Braid, ⅝ inch; yard, 10c.; dozen	$1.10
6532	Mercerized Cotton Skirt Braid, 5-yard pieces; each	.15
6533	Taffeta Binding (B. Altman & Co.'s); piece, 15c.; dozen	1.75
6534	Prussian Binding; piece, 18c.; extra quality	.25
6535	Blanket Binding, 1½-inch, cream; yard, 5c.; 2-inch, 7c.; all silk, white or colored, ⅞ inch, 4c.; 1½-inch, 7c.; 2-inch	.11
6536	Belting Silk, double serge; ⅞ inch, yard, 7c.; 1¼-inch	.09
6537	Belting Cotton, grosgrain, 1½ to 3-inch; yard, 8c. to	.13
6538	Elastic, plain silk, 1 inch; yard	.28
6539	Ribbed Silk, 1 inch; fine, yard, 32c.; heavy	.35
6540	Fancy Silk, ruffled; yard, 25c., 40c. and	.60
6541	Silk Loom, white, ⅜, ½ and ⅝ inch; yard, 15c. to	.19
6542	Silk Loom, black, ⅜, ½ and ⅝ inch; yard, 11c. to	.17
6543	Lisle, ¼ to 1 inch; yard, 5c. to	.10
6544	Hat Elastic, silk; black, yard, 5c.; white	.06

Dressing and Hairpins

6545	Pins, English; small size, paper, 10c.; medium, 12c.; large	$ .14
6546	Pins, loose, ½-pound boxes	.25
6547	Pin Books, English; assorted sizes; each	.10
6548	Pin Cubes, large; jet, 13c.; white or colored, 15c.; dull jet	.18
6549	Pin Cubes, small; jet, white or colored	.10
6550	Pearl-head Pins, white or colored; dozen	.08
6551	Safety Pins, Clinton's; small size, dozen, 5c., gross, 50c.; medium, dozen, 6c., gross, 57c.; large, dozen, 6c., gross	.65

Dressing and Hairpins—(Continued)

6552	Steel Safety Pins; dozen, 7c., 8c., 9c.	$ .10
6553	Safety Pins, rolled gold, 2 on card; 15c., 20c.	.22
6554	Collar and Cuff Pins, rolled gold, two on card, 20c.; black	.10
6555	Hairpins, black or brown; straight or waved; paper	.03
6556	Invisible, black, straight or waved; brown, waved; paper	.03
6557	Heavy or invisible, assorted sizes, 100 in box; black only	.09
6558	Heavy gilt or silver; straight or waved, 10c.; invisible, waved	.05
6559	Pin Cabinets, containing safety and hairpins; each	.75
6560	Imitation Shell and Amber Hairpins; per box	.25

Corset and Shoe Laces

6561	Corset Laces, silk, flat; 5 yards, 30c. and 45c.; 6 yards, 35c. and 60c.; 8 yards, 50c. and 75c.; 10 yards, 90c.; 12 yards	$1.10
6562	Corset Laces, silk, tubular; 5 yards, 50c.; 6 yards, 60c.; 8 yards, 75c.; 10 yards, 95c.; 12 yards	1.15
6563	Corset Laces, mercerized, flat or tubular; 6 yards, each, 10c.; 8 yards, 15c.; 10 yards, 18c.; 12 yards	.22
6564	Tie Laces, silk, black, flat; length, ¾ yard, pair, 9c.; 30-inch, 15c.; extra wide, black or tan, 32-inch	.25
6565	Shoe Laces, tubular, with covered tips, mohair; pair, 4c., 5c.,	.06

Hose Supporters, Lindsay's

6566	Plain Silk; pin top, pair, 35c.; with wide elastic	$ .50
6567	Plain Cotton; pin top, pair, 15c.; wide elastic	.20
6568	Misses'; plain silk, pair, 31c.; cotton	.14
6569	Children's; plain silk, pair, 26c.; cotton	.13
6570	Sew On's; wide silk, elastic, front or sides, 40c.; without tabs 35c.; cotton	.25

Hair Nets and Curlers

6571	Hair Nets, round cap shape; white or gray, each, 45c.; colored, each, 20c., dozen	$2.25
6572	Hair Nets; each, 13c., dozen, $1.50; white, 18c., dozen	2.00
6573	Hair Nets, extra size; colored, each, 16c.; dozen	1.75
6574	Hair Nets, all-over size; colored, each, 20c., dozen, $2.25; white, each, 30c., dozen	3.50
6575	Back Nets, silk; each, 4c., dozen	.45
6576	Hair Curlers, kid, 4 to 9-inch; package, 14c., 17c., 22c., 25c., 28c.	.32
6577	Curlers, rubber; card 19c.; magic, 5 on card	.25
6578	Alberta Hair Wavers, aluminum, 6 on card	.25

Scissors

6579	Plain, 4½, 5, 5½ and 6-inch; each, 60c., 70c., 80c.	$ .90
6580	Embroidery; each, 30c., 40c. and	.50
6581	Manicure; 3½-inch, each, 70c.; 4-inch, 80c.; extra fine	1.00
6582	Nail, heavy, 3½-inch; each, 50c.; extra fine	.80
6583	Shears, 6, 7 and 8-inch; each, $1.00, $1.20	1.50

Miscellaneous

6584	Featherbone; silk, yard, 12c.; cotton	$ .09
6585	Collar Featherbone, taffeta; yard, 9c.; wide	.11
6586	Collar Supporters, spiral wire silk or enameled; card	.10
6587	Elastic Shirt Waist Belts; each	.10
6588	Measures, sateen, each, 7c.; in nickel cases, 8c. and	.20
6589	Jewel Bags, cotton, white or gray; each	.50
6590	Folding Coat Hangers, wire; each	.10
6591	Initials, Cash's, single, woven in red; gross, 25c.; double	.20
6592	Names, embroidered on cotton tape, made to order only, time required about ten days; gross, $2.00, half gross	1.25
6593	Safety Belts, white cotton; each, 20c.; all elastic	.25
6594	Sanitary Aprons, medium size; each, 50c. and 65c.; large	.80
6595	Economy Stocking Protectors; card, 15c.; rubber	.10
6596	Emergency Towels, compressed; small, each, 8c., dozen, 90c.; medium, each, 10c., dozen, $1.00; large, each, 12c., dozen	1.30

DRESS SHIELDS

The prices quoted below, except in the four items last given, are for shields of B. Altman & Co.'s exclusive makes, which are guaranteed moisture proof, and in some instances, as noted, are manufactured in a specially desirable shape. In addition, all popular makes can be furnished

		SIZE	PER PAIR	PER DOZ.
6597	Nainsook, double covered, special shape:	2	$ .24	$2.75
		3	.26	3.00
		4	.29	3.25
		5	.35	3.90
		6	.40	4.50
6598	Shirt Waist, nainsook, double covered:	1	.18	2.00
		2	.20	2.25
		3	.26	2.90
	Lace Edge:	2	.29	3.25
6599	Nainsook, double covered, with one short flap:	3	.21	2.40
		4	.24	2.75
6600	Kimono, nainsook, double covered	3	.29	3.25
		4	.32	3.60
		5	.36	4.10

		SIZE	PER PAIR	PER DOZ.
6601	Perfumed Nainsook, double covered:	3	$ .29	$3.25
		4	.32	3.60
6602	Japanese Silk, double covered, special shape:	3	.56	6.50
		4	.60	6.90
6603	Flesh colored Silk, double covered:	3	.45	5.15
		4	.50	5.75
6604	Amolin, double covered, antiseptic:	3	.30	3.30
		4	.33	3.65
		5	.39	4.30
6605	Gem, double covered:	2	.24	2.76
		3	.27	3.12
		4	.30	3.48
		5	.36	4.20
6606	O. M. O.	3	.25	2.88
		4	.28	3.24